THE NUN'S PRIEST'S
PROLOGUE AND TALE

The Cock and the Fox: a misericord in Norwich Cathedral

THE
NUN'S PRIEST'S
PROLOGUE *&* TALE

FROM THE CANTERBURY TALES

BY

GEOFFREY CHAUCER

*Edited with Introduction, Notes
and Glossary by*
MAURICE HUSSEY

CAMBRIDGE
AT THE UNIVERSITY PRESS
1970

Published by the Syndics of the Cambridge University Press
Bentley House, 200 Euston Road, London N.W. 1
American Branch: 32 East 57th Street, New York, N.Y. 10022

Library of Congress Catalogue Card Number: 65–19123
Standard Book Number: 521 04626 2

First published 1965
Reprinted 1970

Printed in Great Britain
at the University Printing House, Cambridge
(Brooke Crutchley, University Printer)

For
JAMES

CONTENTS

The illustration of the Cock and the Fox, taken from a misericord in Norwich Cathedral, is reproduced with the kind permission of Mr James Winny

ACKNOWLEDGEMENTS

My collaborators in the production of this series of books have been ready at all times to assist me in this production of mine. My thanks are due to them and also to Surendra Agarwala for a great deal of help in the preparation of the Glossary. Whenever work of this type has been thrust upon him he has made it appear to be a genuine pleasure to help, no matter at what cost to his own time. F. N. Robinson's complete text of Chaucer's Works is the immediate source of this separate edition but two other editions deserve special mention. Kenneth Sisam's has been before me since I first read *The Nun's Priest's Tale* at school; Nevill Coghill's and Christopher Tolkien's much more recent edition came my way when my own material was in an advanced stage of preparation, but has offered much useful corroboration.

Cambridge   M. P. H.
May 1965

INTRODUCTION

The exuberance and humanity of *The Nun's Priest's Tale*
make it one of the favourite narratives in *The Canterbury
Tales*. So many facets of a popular subject converge in
this single poem, offering so many ideas and appealing at
so many levels, that readers at every stage of sophistication
find a good deal to their taste. Very few modern readers
will abandon it as dull, though many may find that certain
patches of it confound with their obscurity what they might
have clarified. There is a certain mystique in the poem
which reveals itself only gradually and which calls for
comment. On the other hand, there is a ready-made
fascination for all human beings about animal doings.
When an animal is introduced on to a stage human actors
might as well be silent. Ponies, lionesses and otters have all
contributed largely to their modern owners' incomes when
their foibles have been exploited in book form. So too
in the Middle Ages. Chaucer relished bird fables
especially. In *The Parliament of Fowls* he assembled all
species of birds and made them talk; in *The House of
Fame* he allowed himself to be carried off by a large eagle
which is capable of lecturing him and wafting him into the
blue in spite of his weight. That eagle put him down in
another world to study the subjects of all literary inspiration gathered into a single house. *The Nun's Priest's
Tale*, considerably later than these, returns to the house of
birds for inspiration.

Fables of the Fox and the birds were especially popular
in medieval Europe. Those people who could not read
would have heard the stories from minstrels or other

members of minstrels' audiences, and so the tales travelled from one to another, barely needing the permanent record of script. We have below two examples of such stories, told by Aesop and translated and printed by William Caxton in 1484. It is the raw material of *The Nun's Priest's Tale* which is some six hundred lines longer. The first example tells of a Raven eating a piece of cheese which is coveted by the hungry Fox:

They that be glad and joyefull of the praysynge of flaterers oftyme repent them therof, whereof Esope reherceth to us such a fable. A Raven which was upon a tree and held with his bylle a chese, the which chese the Fox desyred moche to have. Wherfore the Foxe wente and preysed hym by suche wordes as folowen: 'O gentyll Raven, thou art the fayrest byrd of all other byrdes. For thy fethers ben so fayr, so bright and so resplendysshynge, and can also so wel synge. Yf thow haddest the voys clere and small, thow sholdest be the moost happy of all other byrdes'. And the foole which herd the flaterynge wordes of the Foxe beganne to open hyr bylle for to synge. And then the chese fylle to the grounde and the Fox toke and ete hit. And when the Raven sawe that for his vayn glorye he was deceyved, waxed hevy sorowfull and repented hym of that he had byleved the Foxe.

There is another version of this fable in which the victim is a partridge. What must be the earliest extant working of this subject in England is represented in the great Bayeux Tapestry. The chief purpose of that work is to portray the landing of the Normans on English soil in 1066, but directly underneath the battle scenes are smaller pictures which add decoration and amusement. A bird in a tree losing a piece of cheese to a fox below is easy to pick out. This pleasant device of matching a heroic tale with an unrelated comic one was familiar to those who copied manuscripts in the Middle Ages and we shall have occasion to return to the theme. When a biblical text had led the eye to the bottom of a page, a group of animals or birds or a cluster of flowers and foliage would take it back up the margin to the top once more, making of the whole page a thing of beauty and not leaving white spaces if invention could fill and enrich them.

The second Aesop fable has the correct animal types:

Oftyme moche talkynge letteth[1] as appiereth by this fable of a Foxe, which came toward a Cocke and sayd to hym: 'I would fayne wete[2] yf thow canst as wel synge as thy fader dyde.' And thenne the Cocke shutte his eyen and beganne to crye and synge. And thenne the Fox toke and bare hym away. And the peple of the towne cryed: 'The Fox bereth away the Cok.' And thenne the Cocke sayd thus to the Foxe: 'My Lord, understandeth thow not what the peple sayth, that thow berest away theyr Cok. Telle to them that it is thyn and not theyrs.' And the Fox said, 'Hit is not yours, but it is myn.' The Cok scaped fro the Foxe mouthe and flough upon a tree. And thenne the Cok sayd to the Fox: 'Thow lyest. For I am theyrs and not thyn.' And thenne the Foxe beganne to hytte erthe both with his mouthe and heed sayenge: 'Mouthe thow has spoken to moche, thow sholdest have eten the Cok, had not be[3] thyn over-many wordes.' And therfor over moche talkyng letteth and to moch crowynge smarteth.[4]

These closely related stories weave together both a comic story and a clear moral purpose. Very few can imagine that it is a tale confined in interest and meaning to chickens and foxes alone: it is so clearly a general moral truth that comes cloaked in feathers and fur.

Once a reader has matured and can follow Chaucer in the original language there are still a few passages that must inevitably prove stumbling-blocks. The rhetorical passages and the digressions were intended for a sophisticated

---

[1] 'is a disadvantage'. [2] 'know'. [3] 'but for'.
[4] 'causes pain'.

audience of medieval courtiers and to bridge the gap between their culture and ours demands a conscious effort. But underneath it all there still stands the oldest and most popular type of narrative, the animal fable. When we realize the richness of the tale we may well wonder where it will stop with its learned subjects and its homespun philosophizing, its dream tales and its general hullabaloo.

Before any aspect of the poem is discussed in greater detail it may be useful to give a brief summary of the contents so that it may be seen at a glance how much of the text is given to narrative and how much to the different digressions and divergences, each of which tells us more about the tale or its teller, the period which produced it or the way in which it would have been interpreted.

SUMMARY

This list may make the Tale look absurdly fragmented. This is not the case. It is left to the individual reader to decide whether there is not a relevance among so many irrelevances, a consistency within so many seeming inconsistencies. In so far as they refer to human problems and predicaments they may be allowed to enhance the Tale rather than to distract from it. The most important elements in this table will be studied in the following pages.

THE TELLER OF THE TALE: THE NUN'S PRIEST

Dominating all three parts of the present Chaucer text is its alleged narrator: the Nun's Priest himself. We know nothing in advance about him: he is barely introduced to us in *The General Prologue*, being seen only as a satellite of the celebrated Prioress:

> Another Nonne with hire hadde she,
> That was hir chapeleyne, and preestes thre.

5

It is commonly allowed that the other two priests were added for the sake of the rhyme and are little more than an oversight on the author's part. This one priest, however, comes alive as the entire poem unfolds, almost as if Chaucer were apologizing for having overlooked him earlier.

As we read *The Canterbury Tales* we are really progressing through two different sorts of poem. The first is the 'foundation' or 'framework' poem, which consists of all the introductory material throughout the entire sequence and includes the link passages which help us, if we wish, to plot the movements of the pilgrims from Southwark down through Kent. The other type of poem is the individual tale. Here again there are numerous subdivisions: the comic, the saint legend, the romance, the miracle, the sermon and the fable. The Nun's Priest, who hardly emerges in *The General Prologue*, assumes distinct imaginative form in his own Prologue and Epilogue and in his Tale as well. There seems to be a projection of the Priest in all three sections which enables us to tell why, when he was asked to entertain the company, he chose an animal fable with human overtones instead of a more overtly serious Morality or saintly life. It is possible, having regard to all these clues, to answer one of the demands that are always made by commentators on these Tales: does the given tale suit its teller? It has usually been assumed that no such criterion applied to this Tale, since so little was known in advance about the Priest.

Many readers, it must be admitted, have failed to build up any picture of the narrator from Chaucer's words. In fact, some young ones have thought that a Nun's Priest might be a woman—a surmise almost encouraged by the picture of him given in the celebrated portrait in the Ellesmere Manuscript of Chaucer. The function of a Nun's Priest could never have been performed by a woman. He had to say Mass daily; he had to administer the sacraments of Penance, Communion and the Extreme Unction of the dying; he had to preach. If a priest could not be engaged to live in the convent permanently, then the services of a member of the local parish clergy had to be sought instead. At the present time, this situation still holds. It is not unknown, either, for a modern priest to find living in a convent surrounded by religious women an irksome form of seclusion from the world at large. The element of irritation with such a life is relevant to our understanding of Chaucer's pilgrim.

It ought to be put on record, however, that a number of modern commentators have disagreed with this interpretation of the work of this celebrated priest. On the evidence of comments upon his muscular nature and his bluff manner it has been suggested that he was only a bodyguard hired to hustle highwaymen out of the path:

> See, whiche braunes hath this gentil preest.   (689)

It can also be said that his horse, 'foule and lene', reflects no credit upon the convent stables if it is a permanent occupant and under the ultimate responsibility of that great animal-lover, Madame Eglentine. Chaucer makes the Host show a lack of respect towards a man in holy orders, though he comes later to accept him as a 'manly man', a man after his own heart by the time the Tale is over. This might support the view that Sir John was only a temporary escort, the 'tough' needed if the ladies were to join the pilgrims at all.

Even these facts can bear a different interpretation. The Prioress has been shown living in a world of fantasy, paying more attention to dogs than to mankind. She would not realize that she was showing disrespect to the Priest by not giving him a better mount when he was riding in her company. Even though she knew him well, she was not a person with the moral discrimination to understand what was happening inside him. A sense of injustice at his social position—the only man in a company of women and probably the only scholar—might prompt him to speak as he does. This is the motive Chaucer offers.

As a subordinate in a nunnery he is also open to the possibly quite unjust charge of immorality which the Host makes at the close:

> Thou woldest ben a trede-foul aright.   (685)

This line suddenly sheds light back upon our recollection of all that had gone before in the narration. The Host's remark may be meant as no more than a coarse compliment, but it could also offend. It is not possible for the Priest to refute it in public and he is either sufficiently pure to resent the charge or sufficiently sensitive to want to avoid an open statement of it. His revenge—and this is what we notice as we read the Tale once more or ponder on it more deeply—takes the form of an animal fable of one male surrounded by seven females, the chief of whom is shown to be practical but stupid. Chaucer developed similar situations when he arranged that the Miller, the Reeve, the Summoner, the Friar and the Canon's Yeoman should all be paying off old and new scores in the tales they told. If we accept it, this aspect of *The Nun's Priest's Tale* gives it new life, and creates a character behind it rather than the mere mouthpiece for the poet which is all that is normally understood to exist.

The suggestive line quoted from the Host would mean that the Priest has made one or more of the nuns his mistress, so that we catch an echo of line 101:

> Whiche were his sustres and his paramours.

In its context the line refers to the natural morality of the barnyard, but if we look a little more closely it yields a further interpretation. The 'sustres' might even be identifiable under such names as Sister Mary, Sister Elizabeth or Sister Genevieve rather than Pertelote, Pinte or any other name associated with real or legendary medieval hens. Such a reference to the speaker's domestic circumstances, once followed, cannot be blotted out. The cock at once becomes a figure akin to the Priest, a projection of him, and if the Tale is not a hint of his own sexual practices, it may be a revelation of his suppressed desires, or at the very least an exasperated comment on an irritating situation. Undeniably it is a tale of a clever male surrounded by stupid females, and the teller would know how to apply it to the unspecified convent whose Prioress spoke only the French of a suburb of London.

Yet more substance is given to this interpretation if the portrait of the Prioress herself in *The General Prologue* is studied once more. Everybody familiar with it will recall the account of her table-manners:

> Ne wette hir fingres in hir *sauce* depe.

This comes back to mind when the meal-table of the anonymous widow in the Priest's narrative is described:

> Of poynaunt *sauce* hir neded never a deel.   (68)

On that cottage table the fare is of the plainest with *broun breed*, which has the connotations of poverty sometimes associated today with black bread. The Prioress, on the other hand, used the best white bread, called *wastel*, as a dog-food. The widow suffers real poverty:

litel was hir catel and hir rente   (61)

where the Prioress can be described as 'wedded to poverty' only by a pious old fiction of the Church.

Such contrasts point to a possible plan operative outside the foundation poem and the individual tale, which allows the reader to find the satire out for himself. In this way it seems very likely that Chaucer was repairing his early omission in a subtle manner, allowing us to relate the teller to the Tale if we wish and providing a consistency which stands up to our inspection.

THE TALE OF THE TELLER: 'THE NUN'S PRIEST'S TALE'

The pilgrims had been nearing Rochester and about half-way to Canterbury when the Monk began his Tale. It had been assumed, from the look of the man, that he would tell a jovial story, possibly one about horses and hounds. In fact, his contribution was a series of short stories from classical, biblical and other sources which confirmed the seriousness of human problems and proved the truth of his opening definition of tragedy:

> Tragedie is to seyn a certeyn storie,
> As olde bookes maken us memorie,
> Of him that stood in greet prosperitee,
> And is yfallen out of heigh degree
> Into miseries, and endeth wrecchedly.

The listeners were growing restless because there seemed to be no end to his examples and no unity in them other than the moral, which served only to depress them. More to their taste had been the comic view of life of the Wife of Bath. She had shirked some of the regrets in her existence but she placed beside them a radiant acceptance of the joys of life:

> But Lord Crist, whan it remembreth me
> Upon my yowthe, and on my jolitee,
> It tikleth me aboute myn herte roote.
> Unto this day it dooth myn herte boote
> That I have had my world as in my time.

Certainly there are limitations in her outlook: her world and time are contracting and she has little to provide a suitable resource for her future. Yet we are, as a race, given to superficiality, we can bear very little reality, and it was Chaucer's task to provide for both the comic and the tragic visions of human existence. As soon as the Monk has completed his account of the hanging of Croesus, the Knight interrupts the recital and the Host backs up his noble patron.

The Nun's Priest, invited to hold forth next, presents a Tale which keeps its tragic elements under control and resolves them in a comic climax. Some critics stress the tragedy in the Tale, as if it were an appendix to the Monk's recital, but once we reduce the sorrows of Greece, Troy, Rome and Carthage to the immediate context of a farmyard they lose at once. Just as the Cock and the Hen find it difficult to crowd side by side on their narrow perch, comedy and tragedy cannot co-exist for too long without one edging the other off. It seems as though

Chaucer has the two in a nice balance most of the time during this Tale, but the resolution, which seems serious, is really comic and forbids tears.

The main plot has been outlined already in the two Aesop fables. First of all it is the poet's task to establish the shadowy character of the widow and her daughters, adding a sketch of their home which is also the hall where Chauntecleer and Pertelote have their perch. Whereas the Cock is a prince among cocks and a lion among birds, the humans in comparison are both poor and lowly. Yet they have a contented life and offer no targets for tragedy. They are the agricultural working classes, counterparts of Chaucer's Plowman, capable of leading the good life without ostentation or pride. In these respects they are perfect foils for the Cock, who imagines himself a member of the nobility of his race and nearly loses his life for his vanity.

The Cock's dream, with which the plot opens, immediately exposes a hollowness in him. He is, for all his haughty demeanour, extremely scared, though once the Fox makes the near-fatal onslaught Chauntecleer regains his composure and courage. We should notice the close interlinking of two incidents. Chauntecleer, like his dead father, has to be tempted to close his eyes and blind himself to his grave danger; Russell the Fox has to be flattered into opening his mouth to release his victim. Two episodes move into closer relation: if only each of them had kept his mouth shut nothing could have gone wrong. It is a criticism of speaking out of turn. Whether the moral is for birds not to take so much pleasure in crowing or for humans not to boast and brag, the story neatly accomplishes its purpose:

Thou shalt namoore, thurgh thy flaterye,
Do me to singe and winke with myn ye;
For he that winketh, whan he sholde see,
Al wilfully, God lat him nevere thee.   (663–6)

Aesop's Raven fable and Cock fable are united to make two points: keep alert and do not talk too much.

The noisy pandemonium which accompanies the closing scene gives great pressure and vitality to the verse and increases the volume at which the moral is delivered. It seems that the whole village is rushing past and shouting, anxious for the Cock's deliverance and the Fox's defeat. In the end, what looked like being a tragedy is no more than a chastisement or a rude and sobering shock to complacency. For the Cock it is a 'fortunate fall' and because he is basically a wise fellow he has learned his lesson.

Thus, very briefly, the story can be recounted. What remains—and there is indeed a great deal of it—is the personal mechanics of one narrator's way of working through the story. It is lengthened with digressions and rhetorical flourishes which proclaim his delight in his task, and continue further and further until the story assumes apparently epic proportions. Its final effect is achieved when a balanced reading of human life is secured, neither too comic nor too tragic but exactly poised between the two.

THE NARRATOR'S DIGRESSIONS

(i) *Dreams*

The first digression in the Tale arises immediately from the opening incident and turns primarily upon a topic of general and perpetual interest: can dreams tell the truth?

Today if we are worried by dreams it may be because they foretell the truth (precognitive dreams) or because they contain highly symbolic episodes which tell the truth about personality disorders. Where we might enlist the help of a psychiatrist, a medieval man might have turned to a priest or a physician.

It is typical of the academically trained medieval mind that it should tackle such a teasing problem as dreaming by the aid of a long-established author as an 'auctoritee', and that the result should emerge in the form of a long list of propositions and alternatives. Cicero's thoughts upon the dream of Scipio Africanus attracted the attention of a later commentator and analyst named Macrobius whose views were accepted by Chaucer and many others.

Macrobius turned his attention to precognitive or prophetic dreams. He recognized three categories. First, there were those in which the future is precisely revealed. Chauntecleer's dream is a perfect example of this type, right down to the colour of the marauder. Secondly, there were those in which the future was revealed in a symbolic form that still needed interpretation. Finally, there were dreams which contained a direct voice and warning, ignored at one's cost. The threefold vision that occupies Chauntecleer's first dream-legend fits into this category.

Baser, grotesque or insignificant dreams were also divided into two classifications. First, there are those illogical experiences in which no significant line of development can be detected. There is something of this in the dream of the hunt in Chaucer's *Book of the Duchess*. Secondly, there are nightmares that have often been interpreted as the results of indigestion. Scrooge in

Dickens's *Christmas Carol* believed that one of his ghostly visitors was the result of a piece of undigested cheese. Pertelote writes off her husband's prophetic dream as an experience of a similar order.

Other medieval writers favoured a totally different form of analysis. For them the interesting ones were those that extended the operation of things done in the course of the day. For example, we may dream of some book we have been reading, or the continuation of a physical activity of which the muscles themselves seem to retain a memory. There is also the dream of intellectual work in which the subconscious mind seems to be solving problems it had not worked out in the daytime; or the dream of a wish-fulfilment in which a daytime activity is followed to a more pleasing conclusion than real life has yet reached. Medieval doctors believed that all dreams, apart from the prophetic or celestial type, were the result of a temporary imbalance in the humours of the body, whether of choler, phlegm, blood or black bile, which are the four elements that made up the entire medieval world of physiology, psychology and medicine. Pertelote may have been wrong in her diagnosis of her husband's dream, but she showed herself well informed of medical practice of her day.

The problem still remains: was Chauntecleer right to interpret his dream as a prophecy or was Pertelote right in scenting only an animal explanation? The fable provides the answer, but Chaucer had had such problems in mind many years. He wrote a series of dream visions, *The Book of the Duchess*, *The House of Fame* and *The Parliament of Fowls*, each of which is comparable in some way with the dream episodes we are discussing. The first of these poems has already been mentioned. The second opens with an extended passage which is immediately relevant:

> God turne us every drem to goode!
> For hit is wonder, be the roode,
> To my wit, what causes swevenes[1]
> Either on morwes or on evenes;[2]
> And why th'effect folweth of somme,
> And of some hit shal never come.

The whole of the *Proem* could well be consulted. Here is one more passage from it:

> Or if that spirites have the might
> To make folk to dreme a-night;
> Or if the soule, of propre kinde,
> Be so parfit, as men finde,
> That it forwot that is to come,
> And that hit warneth alle and some
> Of everich of her aventures,
> Be avisiouns or be figures.

It would be extremely convenient if one could call one of these categories a *dreme* and the other a *swevene* but it does not seem that the words were strictly defined in Chaucer's day. What is undoubted is that Chauntecleer and Pertelote each represent one view upon a burning topic of debate, and that Chaucer had again tackled a problem he had left behind in his three love visions. We cannot call the Hen ignorant: she means her advice for the best and she is well informed. It merely happened that she was wrong and her husband right. Her identification of red things with choler and black things with melancholy is impressively adroit but also comic at the same time. The simple explanation—a fox who was both red and black—

---

[1] 'dreams'.

[2] 'either on the night after, or the night before [happenings]'.

evades her overcharged simplicity. Her remedy is practical and down to earth:

> For Goddes love, as taak some laxatif.　　　(177)

That superbly intelligent woman, the Wife of Bath, also describes a red dream:

> And eek I seyde I mette[1] of him al night,
> He wolde han slain me as I lay upright,
> And al my bed was ful of verray blood;
> But yet I hope that he shal do me good,
> For blood bitokeneth gold, as me was taught.

The dream is a feigned one, but the interpretation she supplies makes it symbolic: blood equated with gold. Macrobius was prepared for dreams of this variety and, it may be added, so was Freud in his *Interpretation of Dreams* centuries after.

In dwelling so long upon the interpretation of dreams, Chaucer was also reverting to one of the poetic conventions of his day. One of his favourite poems, *Le Roman de la Rose*, was a dream vision; *Piers Plowman* by William Langland and *The Pearl* by an unknown author are two other poems of the fourteenth century in which dream-lore is combined with theological explanation. Dream poetry was a popular device with poets because it was accepted that dreams were capable of capturing greater truths than daytime reasoning and that a vision poem might well be the work of an inspiring agent. By the end of his career as a writer, it is often observed, Chaucer tended to champion the realistic and literal truth. To reduce all the arguments in the books of dream-lore to a debate between a Cock and a Hen is a way of bringing it down to rock-bottom,

---

[1] 'dreamed'.

reducing heroism to mockery, or pretension to a parody of itself. As we have seen, Chauntecleer was correct in his analysis of his own dream but his later behaviour would suggest that he had forgotten it. Nowhere does he see that the Fox was a part of his dream, so that in the end, in spite of the warning, he goes to his fate as if he had had no inkling of it at all. This is both an ironic and a realistic comment on man's concern with foreknowledge.

The Nun's Priest's Tale could have had the effect of challenging its original audience to review the familiar literary convention and think out the problem afresh. If this was the case it would have been one undeniably successful facet of the poem, though only a digression from the narrative. This, in fact, is what it still can be since we are always mystified by some of our dreams and find in them revelations of moments in the future. Macrobius and Chaucer left their readers in awe of a future which was travelling towards them and threw out these visions in advance. Here Chaucer suggests sardonically that the most open hints about the future cannot outweigh human nature and habit.

(ii) *Sermons*

The next digression is more pervasive than the last, springing up in several places in the poem and bearing closely upon the narrator's professional arts. It affects, as a result, not only one or two episodes in the Tale but the handling of the whole narration.

At its highest level, the medieval sermon was an intricate work of verbal art, intellectually gratifying, and studied closely by those who were obliged to persuade others from the pulpit. There are great differences in content between a university sermon preached in Latin and a vernacular one of the same period aimed at a humbler congregation, but they tended to have the same structure or form. We know a good deal about this technique from two books by G. R. Owst, entitled *Preaching in Medieval England* and *Literature and the Pulpit in Medieval England*, of which the second is likely to prove more useful to the student of Chaucer. Examples from several medieval sermons are set down in these books and, if we had nothing else, there is Chaucer's own *Parson's Tale* which is a translation of an authentic French homily against the Seven Deadly Sins.

In all sermons it was necessary to define the terms and the field of operation at the outset. Thus, a biblical text or other theme had to be stated at the beginning and was then slowly broken down into two or three subdivisions, each explained in turn. At this point the popular sermon turned to *examples* which made the point more concretely and memorably. This is exactly what the Nun's Priest is doing in his Tale, carrying over into his story-telling the ways he had learned in a seminary of arranging a more serious form of verbal exhortation. These examples, hereafter called by their Latin name *exempla*, were drawn from biblical, classical and popular learning and slowly brought the preacher to his main point which was the *application* of the sermon's moral. A final emphatic restatement brought the sermon to its end.

Chaucer's *Pardoner's Tale* is more carefully conceived as a sermon than *The Nun's Priest's Tale* and the structure of a typical sermon is a little more closely followed there. Yet it is a sermon on several themes which run together and jostle each other as the speaker reaches out for new types of immorality to expose and punish. In that Tale, too, there are various *exempla*, but our purpose now is to look at the Nun's Priest's technique. We notice how he amasses authorities and introduces themes:

> And forthermoore, I pray yow, looketh wel
> In the Olde Testament of Daniel....
> Reed eek of Joseph...
> Looke of Egipte the King, Daun Parao...
> Lo Cresus...
> Lo heere Andromacha....

It makes no difference that the last two *exempla* are pagan. The development of a sermon needs them for its effect and it cannot be said that the Nun's Priest inundates his hearers with as many authorities as the Pardoner does. Similarly, the Pardoner draws too many morals from his Tale, making it do for so many sinful excesses that it seems to become a vicarious pleasure for him to deliver it, instead of a matter of saddened concern. The Nun's Priest has a solemn moment when he says:

> Mordre is so wlatsom and abhominable....   (287)

There he speaks with the full authority of the Church behind him.

It is not the purpose of the Nun's Priest to lead people to the better life or to improve them in any ostentatious manner. We accept an exhortation:

> O blisful God, that art so just and trewe   (284)

because a layman could have uttered it. It is more surprising to encounter:

> O Venus, that art goddesse of plesaunce.   (576)

A certain mockery of old pagan ways is permissible. There is even a place where the speaker seems to be blind to his congregation and rushes off at a tangent:

> Allas, ye lordes, many a fals flatour
> Is in youre courtes. (559–60)

The reference to 'ye lordes' is out of place in a predominantly middle-class company, though this does not detract from the truth of his social criticism. He twice uses the formula 'goode men' in the Tale as part of the pulpit manner, and he ends with a reference to St Paul and a blessing as if he has always been accustomed to leaving a platform in this manner.

Such references to the text may serve to vindicate the speaker's professional skill, even where it is inclined to lead him off the track of his narration. Nothing has yet been said about the satire upon sermons and theology which causes further delay. The *exemplum* of St Kenelm provides hearers with a type of pious thought much favoured by the Priest's Nun. Her Tale, in fact, is entirely devoted to the fate of another seven-year-old martyr, and she underlines her most affecting story in pulpit manner. If we turn from *The Prioress's Tale* to the Tale under discussion, we find that Kenelm was not too good to be true. He dreamed the warning vision and his nurse interpreted it accurately, but he was too young to understand that his sister was likely to have him murdered:

> but he nas but seven yeer oold,
> And therfore litel tale hath he toold.... (351–2)

In other words he is a perfectly normal child. Other speakers, the Priest implies, sermonize too much and the Church has an endless repertory of child-saint stories, each of them fitted to a particular age, each precocious and cut out for sentimental sermons. In comparison, the handling of St Kenelm is brief and matter-of-fact.

Satire upon ecclesiastical practices reaches its height in the digression upon Predestination. Since the abduction of Chauntecleer was heralded by dream-warnings, the Tale suggests that the future must be charted out and planned in order that revelations and warnings can be sent at all. In this lies a problem still unsolved. The Christian view of life, as we know it today, rests upon the concept that man is free to choose his own path and that God's understanding of his capacities and desires does not force him to make one choice. In the Middle Ages the Church's position was not fully defined. Some writers held that divine foreknowledge was also divine compulsion and that human beings were not free to make their own way. The three authorities mentioned in the poem (St Augustine, Boethius and Bradwardine) all held distinct views and Chaucer's point in referring to them is to satirize a lack of common policy. It has not been said whether the speaker of this passage is the Cock, the Nun's Priest or Chaucer himself because it is extremely difficult to decide which of these three persons is the spokesman at this or any other of several points in the story. Is it a cock, a priest, or a poet doubting the competence of a human organization? Is it a man thinking that for a divinely instituted organization the Church is oddly tentative in its teaching? Should there have been these differences of opinion on this matter at all? These questions are never answered because it would be undiplomatic to do more than glance in their direction. It is likely that Chaucer thought members of the Church should be both competent and free to discuss such theological issues, but he doubted their capabilities and meant the poem to have an anti-clerical twist to it.

A conventional interpretation of the fall of Chauntecleer would have been that vanity and pride were responsible. Yet when the climax of the Tale is reached the theologian is for a moment silent. Nothing is heard about making the punishment fit the crime or the wages of sin. All that is given is a complaint to a classical deity:

> O Venus, that art goddesse of plesaunce... (576)
> Why woldestow suffre him on thy day to die? (580)

Plesaunce, meaning 'sensuality', becomes a desirable way of life. Is it the priest speaking or the poet?

I believe that the Nun's Priest was created in order to allow the poet to express some of his dissatisfactions with the Church, and that the Church's own techniques of sermon-building provided him with a most useful and appropriate weapon. He appears to be implying that one might as well be a pagan if the Christian message is as indistinctly transmitted and as unauthoritative as it seems to be upon the question of predestination. In fact, one might see this Tale as a part of the debate, often held in the medieval universities, upon whether the pagans were saved without the benefit of Christianity. We should not forget, though, that we are reading a poem and not a tract and it is for the poet to deploy his materials appropriately. This I believe he does by his showing at one point a Christian text and at another a pagan one. Thus, we have:

> Redeth Ecclesiaste of flaterye (563)

(although the reference is to the wrong book of the Bible) and on the other hand the meditation on the fact that

> on a Friday fil al this meschaunce. (575)

A perfect way, it seems, to show the changing ideas in the mind of a dissatisfied and probably rebellious cleric. Only the technique of digression could make the point so subtly and well.

(iii) *The byways of rhetoric*[1]

To be a successful writer in the Middle Ages it was not enough to have certain experiences to set down. It was essential to understand the different techniques with which the experiences were to be handled. As Chaucer's Squire puts it:

> Myn Englissh eek is insufficient,
> It moste been a rethor excellent.

A *rethor* is one who professed rhetoric, the art of elegant and persuasive writing. All the ideas of composition taught in schools today might be termed 'rhetoric', but in former times the technical aspect of the study was a great deal more detailed. The ultimate models in the Middle Ages and afterwards were the Romans Cicero and Quintilian, but their views were filtered through a number of other writers such as Geoffroi de Vinsauf whom we find mentioned by the Nun's Priest.

The student found so many rules governing the art of composition that a successful copyist could seem a greater artist than a more impatient writer with something original to offer. There was very little left which could possibly surprise the reader as convention after convention was exploited in a long work. This is not to decry great writers whose use of convention is so successful, so clearly related to the handling of direct experience, that we are unaware of the existence of a conventional rule in the

[1] Further information upon medieval rhetoric appears in *An Introduction to Chaucer*, ch. 4.

work. There were conventions that suggested methods of heightening and colouring the utterance, such as repetitions, metaphors and similes, allegory and innuendo, and many more. A true author found his wings and flew over them all, but a student would need to turn to such a book as Vinsauf's *Nova Poetria* where models for all manner of poems were given. It will be seen from the title that the work was in Latin: the examples were in Latin too, and one valid criticism of the rules of rhetoric is that they were based upon models in an alien tongue and proposed standards of taste at variance with the nature of the English language. In Chaucer's case we may say that his earlier poems owe more to literary conventions than his later ones, and that from being a reader and student of Vinsauf he progressed to being one of his critics.

In *Nova Poetria* there are Latin poems to fit such situations as 'a person elated in prosperity'. A novice would be invited to study this model and then use it for a modern example. Other models are labelled 'an arrogant person' and 'one frightened in adversity'. Vinsauf could not have foreseen that his models would have been used to explain the state of a cockerel's mind or to underline the epic significance of farmyard activities. The following lines:

> For evere the latter ende of joy is wo.
> God woot that worldly joye is soone ago (439–40)

are appropriate for the death of a monarch, yet in *The Nun's Priest's Tale* they are inspired by the rape of Chauntecleer. Immediately after this couplet Chaucer continues:

> And if a rethor koude faire endite,
> He in a cronicle saufly mighte it write
> As for a sovereyn notabilitee. (441–3)

Until it is realized what Chaucer is doing in these three lines they must seem an irrelevant aside, one of many in the Tale. Chaucer is in fact summing up the earlier couplet as the work of a *rethor* and directing his readers to a parody at work in it. Vinsauf in his book of rhetoric provided a model appropriate for a 'person elated in prosperity fallen low' and Chaucer was obviously rather proud of his burlesque of it.

We owe to Nevill Coghill and Christopher Tolkien the discovery of the section in *Nova Poetria* concerning the description of a typical heroine: 'let the whole description be polished to the toe-nail'. This is the starting-point for Chaucer's description of Chauntecleer, to the very last detail:

> Lik asure were his legges and his toon;
> His nailes whitter than the lilie flour. (96–7)

Similarly, the addresses to Venus, to Destiny and the interjection of 'O woful hennes', even the very idea of frequent digression: all these are parodies of the celebrated rhetorician.

The best known piece of borrowing is from the Complaint upon the death of Richard I:

> O Gaufred, [Geoffroi de Vinsauf] deere maister soverain,
> That whan thy worthy King Richard was slain
> With shot, compleynedest his deeth so soore,
> Why ne hadde I now thy sentence and thy loore,
> The Friday for to chide, as diden ye? (581–5)

This meditation upon the fate of Richard Coeur de Lion becomes a sly dig at pretentiousness and mannerism in literature. After this topic from English history, Chaucer turns to an exercise in collective classical grief:

> swich cry ne lamentacion,
> Was nevere of ladies maad whan Ilion
> Was wonne. (589–91)

Vinsauf also took up the subject of the miseries of Troy immediately after his treatment of Richard, but in Chaucer's hands it is immediately transformed into a chorus for hens.

The complaint of Hasdrubal's wife at the Fall of Carthage is not a topic in Vinsauf's book, Chaucer derived it from another book he often quoted: St Jerome's attack upon Jovinian.

Historical catastrophes in epic poetry are not in themselves denigrated or minimized by Chaucer's parodies. His target was rhetoricians who preferred the careful use of a model to a sensitive handling of emotions and experiences of all types. A defence of the true art of poetry lies at the heart of all the digressions that we have cited, so that they are no longer irrelevant, but rather the play of wit on the poet's part, difficult as it may be for us to discover this at our first reading. In some of them Chaucer the poet is more prominent than Sir John the Priest whose professional skills were discussed in the last section. Once more we are led to ask whether it is the narrator or the poet who is responsible for a given passage in the poem. Here it is the poet, for the movement of thought is that of the entire poem and all of a piece with it: finding out a form of writing that can assist in a parody; using it to reduce solemnity and pomposity to laughter; yet without destroying the due seriousness of a topic and without offending against the criteria of good taste, sense, or morality.

THE NARRATOR AS POET

In spite of the importance of rhetoric as an academic subject with long-lasting effects upon literary practitioners, it is not to be forgotten that several unsophisticated types

3-2

of writer could afford to ignore what was in rhetoric books. Those who composed and repeated ballads and folksongs were more interested in the human situations than in rhetoric. It is good to keep ballad and folksong in mind, because they are examples of a spoken or sung art, only written down because we have an urge to preserve them. Chaucer was like the balladists in one way at least: he wrote his poetry to be declaimed; he is shown in a picture reading his work aloud to a group of listeners. The speed at which one can comprehend new material through the ear alone is limited. The eye can return to a line forgotten or not understood, but not the ear. Thus, although in recent years the public recitation of new poetry has become a familiar form of entertainment, it is certain that, to the ear alone, highly complex writing (like the poetry of Dylan Thomas, for instance) becomes more of a pattern of successful sounds and isolated images than a perfectly comprehended whole.

Complex metaphors such as we are accustomed to finding in Shakespeare and his contemporaries are generally absent from the poetry of Chaucer. There may be double meanings and puns occasionally, but simple analogies and similes are more frequent. We are likely to find a figurative statement as simple as:

> Taketh the fruit and lat the chaf be stille.

Or a throwaway image like this:

> If he wol serve thee, rekke nat a bene.

It might be possible to comment solemnly upon the worthlessness of beans in Chaucer's England but it is better not to run behind the poet making comments of this unhelpful type. We should respect the fact that these conventional phrases, simple allusions and illustrations are there to suit the speed of thought and range of reference of the members of the audience. It may be difficult at first for us to do this if we have studied the literary criticism of recent years. Earlier in the present century, critics favoured the idea that a poem was an 'organic growth' which was the one single and inevitable way of making a new experience concrete and verbal. Such an idea is more helpful, perhaps, than the methods of other critics who define the success of a poem as the outcome of a tension of words and phrases full of ambiguities, where the overall structure of a poem may sometimes exist at variance with individual phrases in it. We can of course use either the former approach, which is nearer to the simpler notions of art in the romantic sense, or the latter, which makes a poem into a structure or a shape, a work of architecture rather than a fluid inspiration. Either method is likely to make heavy weather of a medieval poem which is ready to communicate to its reader much more easily, provided that there is no language barrier between the poet and his audience.

A simple approach can turn to a poetic couplet like the following and appreciate it:

> For evere the latter ende of joy is wo.
> God woot that worldly joye is soone ago. (439–40)

We have already seen what is meant if we call this in itself a conventional observation. The phrase *God woot* does little more than encourage a mood of acceptance in the hearer. The concept of joy appears twice in eight words and receives the emphasis which a preacher might give it in a sermon; it sinks in very swiftly because the thought-range of the couplet is carefully restricted. Sometimes a notion is repeated immediately:

> I conseille yow the beste, I wol nat lie. (179)

The listener can afford a momentary withdrawal of his full attention so that he returns to a more active participation in the next idea:

> That bothe of colere and of malencolie. (180)

He is obliged to switch his attention on again for the two nouns in that line.

Above all, Chaucer was seeking out the natural pace of thought for his verse and turning to familiar diction in order to make his task easier:

> And certes in the same book I rede,
> Right in the next chapitre after this—
> I gabbe nat, so have I joye or blis. (298–300)

It will also be discovered that the end of this Tale is full of a kind of 'action-writing' which runs most easily off the tongue because of its alliteration:

> Of *b*ras, they *b*roghten *b*emes, and of *b*ox,
> Of horn, of *b*oon, in whiche they *b*lewe and powped,
> And therwithal they shriked and they howped. (632–4)

This passage comes alive with its onomatopoeia, it re-enacts the furious pace of the chasing villagers in the way the mouth has to manipulate the consonants in it. The entire passage is a particularly splendid example of vigorous, masculine language, direct and without digression. One image intensifies it greatly:

> They yolleden as feendes doon in helle. (623)

It will be recalled that a great quantity of English poetry written in the Middle Ages did not use rhyme at all, but employed alliteration as its technique. The poem *Piers Plowman*, for instance, is written in this manner without rhyme, and it was natural for Chaucer to fall back upon the older technique occasionally in his writings even though he nowhere relies upon it exclusively. Rhyme was a newer form, and it is sometimes objected that Chaucer inserts a final word into a line only because of the rhyming. This may indeed be the case and there are occasions in his work when his rhyme-words may cause us a little discomfort. Here is an example:

> After the opinioun of certein clerkis.
> Witnesse on him that any parfit clerk is   (469–70)

or again:

> Allas, and konne ye been agast of swevenis?
> Nothing, God woot, but vanitee in sweven is. (155–6)

It is probable that French poetry could have taken this in its stride in the Middle Ages and that English rhyming had not yet grown as subtle as it became in later centuries. To inveigh against a clumsiness of technique here is to be preoccupied with minor details.

On occasions, Chaucer also seems to ignore the desire for a normal iambic line of ten syllablles when he is fully extended by his subject. Here, for instance, is the way in which he captures physical speed:

> Ran cow and calf, and eek the verray hogges,
> So fered for the berking of the dogges.   (619–20)

An urgent message is given still greater force in a longer line without detracting from the comprehension:

> Pekke hem up right as they growe and ete hem in. (201)

In all these cases it is the discerning ear that is the judge. Does it sound well, does it convey its meaning by the ear? This is what a medieval audience, deprived of a page of script, would have felt above everything else. We who are fed on a surfeit of print, and may sometimes be gladdened at the sight of a poem standing alone on a page with white space all round it, can often forget the requirements of an older generation.

In everything that follows we are to consider the wider effects of the poetry, since we have seen that the verse is not devised to yield the utmost only to close critical scrutiny.[1] In his excellent study *Chaucer and the French Tradition*, Charles Muscatine compares Chaucer's art with that of the visual artist of the medieval or Gothic period. He shows that visual artists were attracted to the principle of juxtaposition: putting one subject beside another, as in the great series of sculptures found flanking the portals of cathedrals. In them person after person is arranged in order. Similarly, scene after scene occurs in a Chaucer Tale and the reader's art is to find out the connexion of ideas that links them. The classical figures in the different *exempla* form one group, the cock and hens another. The technique of cross-reference throws each into fresh perspective. Nobody can think that the Falls of Troy or Carthage are themselves ridiculed by the nearness of the fall of Chauntecleer. It is the latter that is diminished by the contrast, if we believe that Chauntecleer himself saw his own fate blown up to epic dimensions.

In the eighteenth century Alexander Pope used a similar technique. *The Rape of the Lock* is a tale about cutting off

[1] See, however, as exception to this lines 474–5 and the note upon them.

a lock of hair, but the grand title would encourage one to think of *The Rape of Lucrece* or some other incident of a tragic order. The purpose of the juxtaposition, once we see it, is not to ridicule a classical tragedy but to make a slightly affectionate mockery of the triviality of the people of Pope's own world, who think it an event of major significance. At the heart of Pope's satire there is the desire to elevate and then deflate the pretentious by the technique of the mock-heroic. It is the same technique that controls our full response to *The Nun's Priest's Tale*. A poetic effect of this type needs the whole range of a poem to show itself; it can rarely be compressed neatly into a single word, image or line. Classical references in Pope or Chaucer sometimes need sentences to unfold and when they have unfolded they give the poetry a metaphorical quality without precisely supplying it. The irony and the allusion are sufficiently broad as figures of speech to communicate to listeners who might lose the complex force of poetry of more closely-wrought texture.

A fine example of this poetic effect comes in the way Chaucer introduces the Widow on the one hand and the Cock on the other. The technique is one of surprise. In the description of the Widow we find a number of negatives which hint at her deficiencies, while in the description of the Cock Chaucer provides a number of positives. We may perhaps put two extracts together. Firstly of the Widow:

> Ful sooty was hire bour and eek hir halle,
> In which she eet ful many a sklendre meel. (66–7)

A lady's bower demands a romantic setting with knights and scenes of love. *Sooty* dispels all this at one blow. The

word *sklendre* then applies to both the meal and the hall.
In Vinsauf's study of rhetoric this device was called
oppositio. Against it let us place Chauntecleer, whose

> coomb was redder than the fyn coral,
> And batailled as it were a castel wal.   (93–4)

He stands up to comparison and exceeds it: he is associated
with the battlements of a castle inside which there would
have been room for several spacious halls and bowers.

Another example of unexpected association occurs when
Chauntecleer is viewed with his seven mistresses. Pertelote, his favourite, is the fine lady of the tradition of courtly
romance, whose human counterparts were wooed by
knights suffering the *peyne* of passion. To find such
allusions in a beast fable is unparalleled, but nevertheless
the two traditions complement each other to enrich the
meaning of the whole work. In studying such devices as
these we have left the study of rhetoric for a living form
of art that needs an alert reader to do it justice. Com-
pression of metaphor is no part of this technique, for only
the broadest devices, that can succeed when they are
heard but once aloud, are suitable for medieval narrative.

THE NARRATOR AS MORALIST

Even when we have understood all these aspects of the
Tale there remains a problem. Does this Tale mean more
than it says? It is simple in its basic fable, but what an
enormous number of important topics have been saluted
as the poem unfolds! Tragedy, rhetoric, scholarship,
ecclesiastical authority, science, medicine, simple domesti-
city and courtly love all play their part in making it a

universal poem in miniature. At the end there come these challenging lines:

> Taketh the moralite, goode men.
> For Seint Paul seith that al that writen is,
> To oure doctrine it is ywrite, ywis;
> Taketh the fruit, and lat the chaf be stille.   (674–7)

This is the passage that has set the commentators to work. Has Chaucer got something up his sleeve?

One after another, scholars have come forward with their individual and irreconcilable insights into the story. While for some it is only a fable against flattery, vanity or complacency, for others it is much more intricate. The widow, for instance, has been said to depict the state of the Church about 1400: implying that it was in rather a poor way. The Fox, because he was often shown in pictures and carvings as a preacher, wily and treacherous, has been interpreted of late as a symbol of the orders of Friars who were snatching the living away from the Poor Parsons. In this reading the Cock (with seven incestuously connected partners) becomes a typical, though somewhat lax, parish priest. Such an allegory can only be sustained by seizing upon a partial truth and forgetting all the rest. The Tale may be interpreted, I believe, in ecclesiastical terms but much more simply: it expresses the attitude of a convent priest, dissatisfied with his lot, a confessor who knows a good deal to the discredit of the nuns and who yet says with heavy irony:

> I kan noon harm of no womman divine.   (500)

The reference to St Paul about *al that writen is* refers only to all that is written in the *Scriptures* and not to everything that has ever been written down. To go a long way

35

into moralizing is to run counter to the words of the great Dominican, St Thomas Aquinas. He points out that the Bible (and the Church in expounding the Bible) may treat of incidents in various figurative ways because it is God's word. Secular writing was a different matter altogether. 'In no intellectual activity of the human mind can there properly speaking be found anything but the literal sense.' His writings have always been treasured by the Church and his name revered as one of the most authoritative of all. It is also quite true that churchmen would use animal fables and pursue them to the bounds of allegorical absurdity. We do not readily equate an elephant with the ordinary mortal, but in one medieval sermon a legend is recalled in which the elephant is caught, as he leans against a tree, by a trapper who saws halfway through the tree-trunk. Falling over as the tree collapses, he is unable to rise because he has no knee-joints. The theme is based upon a common mistaken notion about elephant anatomy and it was offered as an image of divine truth to show how the Devil makes snares for unsteady Christians. The allegory was probably allowed, but with groans from some who heard it explained. A Fox fable, on the other hand, delivered as an entertainment to a company of travellers, has no such privileged status. To expound the situation of Chauntecleer as a symbol of the human soul is an 'intellectual activity of the human mind' which is based upon another one without the informed truth of divine inspiration behind it at any point.

One aspect of the Fox legend mentioned before is now ready to be further examined here. We know that Fox stories were common throughout Europe and may throw light upon European popular culture in the Middle Ages.

In England the legends appear more often in pictorial than in verbal form. In France the case is different. The *Fables* by Queen Marie of France and the anonymous fox-epic, *Le Roman de Renard*, set them down at considerable length. In England, though, we turn to carvings in churches, upon pillars or on bosses in the roof; and lastly on the undersides of the tip-up seats known as misericords. The frontispiece shows the Fox running away with his victim chased by Malkin with her distaff and it comes from Norwich Cathedral. The same scene appears in other churches as evidence of its popularity.

In manuscripts, too, especially in England, there are many foxes among the comic and grotesque creatures that fill up the margins of the pages. One manuscript page shows a duck being carried off by a fox and the word 'Quek', exactly as in a modern strip-cartoon, is found coming from his mouth. Another Fox picture shows him as a bishop preaching to a varied company of birds. Reynard became a favourite symbol of hypocrisy or figure of pure fun. In a series of pictures that remind one of the rhyme 'Who killed Cock Robin?' all the individual animals are shown preparing for the funeral of the Fox, and in one carving at the church in Brent Knoll in Somerset the Fox is shown hanging on a rope, distinctly dead, before the funeral ceremonies. A Fox cannot be a corpse and a devil-symbol at the same time, since the devil will always have the cunning to evade his pursuers. Is a Fox, even with a Cock in his mouth, the same symbol all the time? Can he possibly be a rascally friar threatening to oust the parish clergy, a devil, and a corpse? It is dangerous to make symbolic identifications too simply.

There is one further appearance of the Fox to record.

In the fourteenth-century Ormesby Psalter, now at Oxford, there is an illuminated page of great interest. At the top there is the text of the scene in which the priests of Nob are shown in the act of being massacred by order of Doeg (1 Samuel xxii). Slinking off at the foot of the picture, where a grotesque picture might be expected, the copyist of the manuscript displayed Reynard with the captive Cock. This does not make Reynard into a Doeg or encourage us to accept him as a symbol of the killer of priests. It acts upon the reader in a primarily visual manner and it provides for this page of the Bible a perfect example of the mock-heroic principle at work even within a divinely-inspired work. All Fox pictures can be interpreted as realizations of country life, its amusements and its hazards, and as we pass from an epic event to a popular event which mirrors it we should find the mock-heroic rather than diabolic hatred tracking down the noble hero.

The moral of the whole Tale can be expressed in simple terms:

> For he that winketh, whan he sholde see,
> Al wilfully, God lat him nevere thee. (665–6)

> Lo, swich it is for to be recchelees
> And necligent, and truste on flaterye. (670–1)

It is difficult to go much further. One can add that it is an attack upon an ego-centric man who thinks his own fate of world-shaking importance, or upon the complacent man who is horrified by the very idea of pronounced opposition or adversity. The Nun's Priest seems to be leading his hearers to expect more than this. He had, after all, given them his interpretations of Fortune, of the dangers of female counsel, of predestination and the changeableness of life; he had elaborated upon the different types of

dreams. Some people might have called him rather
trivial if he had given only an animal fable: for them he has
perhaps provided food for allegorical surmise. He has also
given a good Tale for those who enjoy no more. With his
dislike of pedantry he probably calculated that some
commentators would make heavy weather of his story, but
still he gives them the opportunity so that they will not
dismiss him as being too light-hearted. Through him
Chaucer was ridiculing those who felt that a story had to
mean more than appeared evident in order to justify its
existence.

All the time we have been considering this Tale we have
probably been uneasily aware of three people narrating it.
One asks, from time to time, is this the poet himself
speaking, the Priest or is it the Cock? Three levels of
meaning are exposed to the view, each one independent of
the other two. Does a Cock explain that he cannot
explain a theological point? Is it Chaucer himself making
criticisms of the Church or is the Nun's Priest? In each
case the interpretation of a point may be slightly altered.
One cannot be sure which it is that is intended at any
given moment. To take the most learned interpretation
and make the poem shine with a professional theologian's
gloss is to make an extremely didactic writer out of Chaucer
and present a poet who looks more like William Langland. To see the poem in this light is to alter it in the
interests of 'high seriousness', a quality which Matthew
Arnold found lacking in Chaucer. To find that in the end
all the most solemn points dissolve into gentle ridicule and
mild irony is much more to the taste of those who see
Chaucer as a wry, satirical character himself and to
remember his own word for himself, 'elvish'. Mock-

heroic is so clearly the means through which a writer can express a subtle unconcern that it suits that elvish image of Chaucer to perfection. If there is indeed in the many digressions of the poem a satire upon pedantic scholars it must inevitably be turned upon those who go too far in their fancy from the innocent summary that he himself gives:

My tale is of a cok, as ye may heere.

THE POET'S SOURCES

What are the literary sources from which Chaucer drew the inspiration for *The Nun's Priest's Tale*? It is a topic on which there is not universal agreement among scholars and it has been debated often in the last sixty years. It no longer seems necessary to spend two-thirds of the Introduction to this Tale upon the subject as it did to Kenneth Sisam over thirty years ago. One answer to the inquiry has already been given in the study of the visual treatment of the Fox legends in the records of medieval English art. For the other we have to turn to continental countries where the Fox legends, as we have already found, took more naturally to the written word.

The French *Le Roman de Renard*, written between 1174 and 1205, is one often-quoted source for Chaucer's Tale. The other is the German version, which is slightly later, called *Reinhardt Fuchs*. It is also possible that Chaucer had the idea from a narrative he had heard, which stood before either of these. The problem inherent in literature which was never written down and has therefore disappeared is as great as that to be found in written work that has since disappeared as well. Chaucer's version is undeniably one where the names have been altered and where the final product is a great deal shorter than the epic treatment accorded to Fox literature in France and Germany.

It is one of the irritating habits of scholars not to allow a creative genius of Chaucer's standing much originality in his handling of old material. While it is of interest to compare a poem with its acknowledged source, a prolonged hunt for unacknowledged sources produces an unbalanced example of literary scholarship. The most satisfactory statement on this source-problem comes from J. R. Hulbert who writes that if there was a direct written source it must have been an abbreviated version 'identical in some respects with the one before the German poet' who wrote *Reinhardt Fuchs*. Quotations from the German poem will be found, with marginal glosses in English, in W. F. Bryan and G. Dempster, *Sources and Analogues of 'The Canterbury Tales'*. Readers will find the material displayed there in greater detail.

However, since *Le Roman de Renard* is a masterpiece in its own right and one of the great animal tales in European literature, we may glance briefly at the episode in it which is closest to Chaucer's Tale. In the French version the two birds, Chauntecleer and Pinte, are kept by a rich farmer. His dream foretells the future but in an indirect manner. He sees not a Fox but an intruder in a red coat whom Pinte identifies correctly as the Fox she has seen lurking outside the farmyard fence. The dreamer himself dismisses the whole notion of a dream-warning and goes to sleep once more. Reynard finding a sleeping victim springs his attack and is unsuccessful. The Cock wakens in time and a great deal of diplomacy is necessary for the Fox to gain his conquest. In this version, too, the Cock crows with his eyes closed and the intruder takes hold of him in the familiar manner. Once more the Cock owes his escape to his brainwave of getting his captor to speak to the following crowd. The final moralization is 'Cursed be the mouth that makes a noise when it should be silent'. Chaucer's Daun Russell makes the same deduction:

> God yeve him meschaunce
> That is so undiscreet of governaunce
> That jangleth whan he sholde holde his pees. (667–9)

There is no hint of any allegorical application of the fable and the episode closes.

From so brief a summary we can perhaps judge how original Chaucer was in his handling of the theme. No other treatment of it subjects it to the vast and almost universal inspection that we have been studying or turns it into the central text in a mock-sermon upon the follies and vanities of mankind. To hunt persistently for sources or allegorizations takes the student further and further from the text of Chaucer. Such interpretations appear surprisingly pedantic when it is recalled that it is only a Fox legend. It would be the same if a modern literary critic were to insist upon an improbable psychological interpretation of a nursery rhyme.

Note. In connexion with the Introduction readers may be referred to the companion volume in the present series, *An Introduction to Chaucer*, in which several topics are discussed at greater length. References to this book will also be found in the Notes at the back of this text.

NOTE ON THE TEXT

The text which follows is based upon that of F. N. Robinson (*The Complete Works of Geoffrey Chaucer*, 2nd ed., 1957). The punctuation has been revised, with special reference to the exclamation marks. Spelling has been partly rationalized, by substituting *i* for *y* wherever the change aids the modern reader and does not affect the semantic value of the word. Thus *smylyng* becomes 'smiling', and *nyghtyngale* 'nightingale', but *wyn* (wine), *lyk* (like), and *fyr* (fire) are allowed to stand.

No accentuation has been provided in this text, for two reasons. First, because it produces a page displeasing to the eye; secondly, because it no longer seems necessary or entirely reliable in the light of modern scholarship. It is not now thought that the later works of Chaucer were written in a ten-syllable line from which no variation was permissible. The correct reading of a line of Chaucer is now seen to be more closely related to the correct reading of a comparable line of prose with phrasing suited to the rhythms of speech. This allows the reader to be more flexible in his interpretation of the line, and makes it unreasonably pedantic to provide a rigid system of accentuation.

NOTE ON PRONUNCIATION

These equivalences are intended to offer only a rough guide. For further details, see *An Introduction to Chaucer*.

SHORT VOWELS

ă represents the sound now written *u*, as in 'cut'
ě as in modern 'set'
ĭ as in modern 'is'
ŏ as in modern 'top'
ŭ as in modern 'put' (not as in 'cut')
final -*e* represents the neutral vowel sound in '*a*bout' or 'attenti*o*n'. It is silent when the next word in the line begins with a vowel or an *h*.

4-2

Note on the Text

LONG VOWELS

ā as in modern 'car' (not as in 'name')

ē (open—i.e. where the equivalent modern word is spelt with
ea) as in modern 'there'

ē (close—i.e. where the equivalent modern word is spelt with
ee or *e*) represents the sound now written *a* as in 'take'

ī as in modern 'machine' (not as in 'like')

ō (open—i.e. where the equivalent modern vowel is pronounced as in 'brother', 'mood', or 'good') represents the sound
now written *aw* as in 'fawn'

ō (close—i.e. where the equivalent modern vowel is pronounced as in 'road') as in modern 'note'

ū as in French *tu* or German *Tür*

DIPHTHONGS

ai and *ei* both roughly represent the sound now written *i* or *y*
as in 'die' or 'dye'

au and *aw* both represent the sound now written *ow* or *ou* as
in 'now' or 'pounce'

ou and *ow* have two pronunciations: as in *through* where the
equivalent modern vowel is pronounced as in 'through' or
'mouse'; and as in *pounce* where the equivalent modern vowel
is pronounced as in 'know' or 'thought'

WRITING OF VOWELS AND DIPHTHONGS

A long vowel is often indicated by doubling, as in *roote* or
eek. The *ŭ* sound is sometimes represented by an *o* as in *yong*.
The *au* sound is sometimes represented by an *a*, especially
before *m* or *n*, as in *cha(u)mbre* or *cha(u)nce*.

CONSONANTS

Largely as in modern English, except that many consonants
now silent were still pronounced. *Gh* was pronounced as in
Scottish 'lo*ch*', and both consonants should be pronounced in
such groups as the following: '*gn*acchen', '*kn*ave', '*word*',
'fo*lk*', '*wr*ong'.

44

THE NUN'S PRIEST'S
PROLOGUE

'Hoo,' quod the Knight, 'good sire, namoore of this!
That ye han seyd is right ynough, ywis,
And muchel moore; for litel hevinesse
Is right ynough to muche folk, I gesse.
I seye for me, it is a greet disese,
Whereas men han been in greet welthe and ese,
To heeren of hire sodeyn fal, allas,
And the contrarie is joye and greet solas,
As whan a man hath been in povre estaat,
And climbeth up and wexeth fortunat,   10
And there abideth in prosperitee.
Swich thing is gladsom, as it thinketh me,
And of swich thing were goodly for to telle.'
'Ye,' quod oure Hooste, 'by Seint Poules belle,
Ye seye right sooth; this Monk he clappeth lowde.
He spak how "Fortune covered with a clowde"
I noot nevere what; and als of a "tragedie"
Right now ye herde, and, pardee, no remedie
It is for to biwaille ne compleyne
That that is doon, and als it is a peyne,   20
As ye han seyd, to heere of hevinesse.
  Sire Monk, namoore of this, so God yow blesse,
Youre tale anoyeth al this compaignye.
Swich talking is nat worth a boterflye,
For therinne is ther no desport ne game.
Wherfore, sire Monk, or Daun Piers by youre name,
I pray yow hertely telle us somwhat elles;

45

For sikerly, nere clinking of youre belles,
That on youre bridel hange on every side,
30 By hevene king, that for us alle dyde,
I sholde er this han fallen doun for sleep,
Althogh the slough had never been so deep;
Thanne hadde your tale al be toold in veyn.
For certeinly, as that thise clerkes seyn,
Whereas a man may have noon audience,
Noght helpeth it to tellen his sentence.
    And wel I woot the substance is in me,
If any thing shal wel reported be.
Sir, sey somwhat of hunting, I yow preye.'
40 'Nay,' quod this Monk, 'I have no lust to pleye.
Now lat another telle, as I have toold.'
Thanne spak oure Hoost with rude speche and boold,
And seyde unto the Nonnes Preest anon,
'Com neer, thou preest, com hider, thou Sir John,
Telle us swich thing as may oure hertes glade.
Be blithe, though thou ride upon a jade.
What thogh thyn hors be bothe foul and lene?
If he wol serve thee, rekke nat a bene.
Looke that thyn herte be murie everemo.'
50   'Yis, sir,' quod he, 'yis, Hoost, so moot I go,
But I be myrie, ywis I wol be blamed.'
And right anon his tale he hath attamed,
And thus he seyde unto us everichon,
This sweete preest, this goodly man, Sir John.

THE NUN'S PRIEST'S TALE

A povre widwe, somdeel stape in age
Was whilom dwelling in a narwe cotage,
Biside a grove, stondinge in a dale.
This widwe, of which I telle yow my tale,
Sin thilke day that she was last a wyf,
In pacience ladde a ful simple lyf,   60
For litel was hir catel and hir rente.
By housbondrie of swich as God hire sente
She foond hirself and eek hir doghtren two.
Thre large sowes hadde she, and namo,
Three keen, and eek a sheep that highte Malle.
Ful sooty was hire bour and eek hir halle,
In which she eet ful many a sklendre meel.
Of poynaunt sauce hir neded never a deel.
No deyntee morsel passed thurgh hir throte;
Hir diete was accordant to hir cote.   70
Repleccioun ne made hire nevere sik;
Attempree diete was al hir phisik,
And exercise, and hertes suffisaunce.
The goute lette hire nothing for to daunce,
N'apoplexie shente nat hir heed.
No wyn ne drank she, neither whit ne reed;
Hir bord was served moost with whit and blak,—
Milk and broun breed, in which she foond no lak,
Seynd bacoun, and somtime an ey or tweye;
For she was, as it were, a maner deye.   80
    A yeerd she hadde, enclosed al aboute
With stikkes, and a drye dich withoute,
In which she hadde a cok, hight Chauntecleer.

In al the land, of crowing nas his peer.
His voys was murier than the murie orgon
On messe-dayes that in the chirche gon.
Wel sikerer was his crowing in his logge
Than is a clokke or an abbey orlogge.
By nature he knew ech ascencioun
90   Of the equinoxial in thilke toun;
For whan degrees fiftene weren ascended,
Thanne crew he, that it mighte nat been
    amended.
His coomb was redder than the fyn coral,
And batailled as it were a castel wal;
His byle was blak, and as the jeet it shoon;
Lyk asure were his legges and his toon;
His nailes whitter than the lilie flour,
And lyk the burned gold was his colour.
This gentil cok hadde in his governaunce
100   Sevene hennes for to doon al his plesaunce,
Whiche were his sustres and his paramours,
And wonder lyk to him, as of colours;
Of whiche the faireste hewed on hir throte
Was cleped faire Damoisele Pertelote.
Curteys she was, discreet, and debonaire,
And compaignable, and bar hirself so faire,
Sin thilke day that she was seven night oold,
That trewely she hath the herte in hoold
Of Chauntecleer, loken in every lith;
110   He loved hire so that wel was him therwith.
But swich a joye was it to here hem singe,
Whan that the brighte sonne gan to springe,
In sweete accord, 'My lief is faren in londe!'
For thilke time, as I have understonde,

48

Maneipl.

Beestes and briddes koude speke and singe.
   And so bifel that in a daweninge,
As Chauntecleer among his wives alle
Sat on his perche, that was in the halle,
And next him sat this faire Pertelote,
This Chauntecleer gan gronen in his throte,   120
As man that in his dreem is drecched soore.
And whan that Pertelote thus herde him roore,
She was agast, and seyde, 'Herte deere,
What eyleth yow, to grone in this manere?
Ye been a verray sleper; fy, for shame.'
   And he answerde, and seyde thus: 'Madame,
I pray yow that ye take it nat agrief.
By God, me mette I was in swich meschief
Right now, that yet myn herte is soore afright.
Now God,' quod he, 'my swevene recche aright,   130
And kepe my body out of foul prisoun.
Me mette how that I romed up and doun
Withinne our yeerd, wheer as I saugh a beest
Was lyk an hound, and wolde han maad areest
Upon my body, and wolde han had me deed.
His colour was bitwixe yelow and reed,
And tipped was his tail and bothe his eeris
With blak, unlyk the remenant of his heeris;
His snowte smal, with glowinge eyen tweye.
Yet of his look for feere almoost I deye;   140
This caused me my groning, doutelees.'
   'Avoy,' quod she, 'fy on yow, hertelees,
Allas,' quod she, 'for, by that God above,
Now han ye lost myn herte and al my love.
I kan nat love a coward, by my feith.
For certes, what so any womman seith,

We alle desiren, if it mighte bee,
To han housbondes hardy, wise, and free,
And secree, and no nigard, ne no fool,
150 Ne him that is agast of every tool,
Ne noon avauntour, by that God above.
How dorste ye seyn, for shame, unto youre love
That any thing mighte make yow aferd?
Have ye no mannes herte, and han a berd?
Allas, and konne ye been agast of swevenis?
Nothing, God woot, but vanitee in sweven is.
Swevenes engendren of replecciouns,
And ofte of fume and of complecciouns,
Whan humours been to habundant in a wight.
160 Certes this dreem, which ye han met to-night,
Cometh of the greete superfluitee
Of youre rede colera, pardee,
Which causeth folk to dreden in hir dremes
Of arwes, and of fyr with rede lemes,
Of rede beestes, that they wol hem bite,
Of contek, and of whelpes, grete and lite;
Right as the humour of malencolie
Causeth ful many a man in sleep to crie
For feere of blake beres, or boles blake,
170 Or elles blake develes wole hem take.
Of othere humours koude I telle also
That werken many a man sleep ful wo;
But I wol passe as lightly as I kan.
    Lo Catoun, which that was so wys a man,
Seyde he nat thus, "Ne do no fors of dremes?"
Now sire,' quod she, 'whan we flee fro the bemes,
For Goddes love, as taak som laxatif.
Up peril of my soule and of my lyf,

50

I conseille yow the beste, I wol nat lie,
That bothe of colere and of malencolie   180
Ye purge yow; and for ye shal nat tarie,
Though in this toun is noon apothecarie,
I shal myself to herbes techen yow
That shul been for youre hele and for youre prow;
And in oure yeerd tho herbes shal I finde
The whiche han of hire propretee by kinde
To purge yow bynethe and eek above.
Foryet nat this, for Goddes owene love.
Ye been ful colerik of compleccioun;
Ware the sonne in his ascencioun   190
Ne finde yow nat repleet of humours hoote.
And if it do, I dar wel leye a grote,
That ye shul have a fevere terciane,
Or an agu, that may be youre bane.
A day or two ye shul have digestives
Of wormes, er ye take youre laxatives
Of lawriol, centaure, and fumetere,
Or elles of ellebor, that groweth there,
Of katapuce, or of gaitris beryis,
Of herbe ive, growing in oure yeerd, ther mery is;   200
Pekke hem up right as they growe and ete hem in.
Be myrie, housbonde, for youre fader kin!
Dredeth no dreem, I kan sey yow namoore.'
   'Madame,' quod he, 'graunt mercy of youre loore.
But nathelees, as touching Daun Catoun,
That hath of wisdom swich a greet renoun,
Though that he bad no dremes for to drede,
By God, men may in olde bookes rede
Of many a man moore of auctorite
Than evere Caton was, so moot I thee,   210

That al the revers seyn of this sentence,
And han wel founden by experience
That dremes been significaciouns
As wel of joye as tribulaciouns
That folk enduren in this lif present.
Ther nedeth make of this noon argument;
The verray preeve sheweth it in dede.

    Oon of the gretteste auctour that men rede
Seith thus: that whilom two felawes wente
220   On pilgrimage, in a ful good entente;
And happed so, they coomen in a toun
Wher as ther was swich congregacioun
Of peple, and eek so streit of herbergage,
That they ne founde as muche as o cotage
In which they bothe mighte ylogged bee.
Wherfore they mosten of necessitee,
As for that night, departen compaignye;
And ech of hem gooth to his hostelrye,
And took his logging as it wolde falle.
230   That oon of hem was logged in a stalle,
Fer in a yeerd, with oxen of the plough;
That oother man was logged wel ynough,
As was his aventure or his fortune,
That us governeth alle as in commune.

    And so bifel that, longe er it were day,
This man mette in his bed, ther as he lay,
How that his felawe gan upon him calle,
And seyde, "Allas, for in an oxes stalle
This night I shal be mordred ther I lie.
240   Now help me, deere brother, or I die.
In alle haste com to me," he saide.
This man out of his sleep for feere abrayde;

But whan that he was wakened of his sleep,
He turned him, and took of this no keep.
Him thoughte his dreem nas but a vanitee.
Thus twies in his sleping dremed hee;
And atte thridde time yet his felawe
Cam, as him thoughte, and seide, "I am now slawe.
Bihoold my bloody woundes depe and wide.
Aris up erly in the morwe tide,   250
And at the west gate of the toun," quod he,
"A carte ful of dong ther shaltow se,
In which my body is hid ful prively;
Do thilke carte arresten boldely.
My gold caused my mordre, sooth to sayn."
And tolde him every point how he was slain,
With a ful pitous face, pale of hewe.
And truste wel, his dreem he foond ful trewe,
For on the morwe, as soone as it was day,
To his felawes in he took the way;   260
And whan that he cam to this oxes stalle,
After his felawe he bigan to calle.

The hostiler answerede him anon,
And seyde, "Sire, your felawe is agon.
As soone as day he wente out of the toun."

This man gan fallen in suspecioun,
Remembringe on his dremes that he mette,
And forth he gooth—no lenger wolde he lette—
Unto the west gate of the toun, and fond
A dong-carte, wente as it were to donge lond,   270
That was arrayed in that same wise
As ye han herd the dede man devise.
And with an hardy herte he gan to crye
Vengeance and justice of this felonye.

53

"My felawe mordred is this same night,
And in this carte he lith gaping upright.
I crye out on the ministres," quod he,
"That sholden kepe and reulen this citee.
Harrow, allas, heere lith my felawe slain.
What sholde I moore unto this tale sayn?
The peple out sterte and caste the cart to grounde,
And in the middel of the dong they founde
The dede man, that mordred was al newe.

O blisful God, that art so just and trewe,
Lo, how that thou biwreyest mordre alway.
Mordre wol out, that se we day by day.
Mordre is so wlatsom and abhominable
To God, that is so just and resonable,
That he ne wol nat suffre it heled be,
Though it abide a yeer, or two, or thre.
Mordre wol out, this my conclusioun.
And right anon, ministres of that toun
Han hent the carter and so soore him pined,
And eek the hostiler so soore engined,
That they biknewe hire wikkednesse anon,
And were anhanged by the nekke-bon.

Heere may men seen that dremes been to drede.
And certes in the same book I rede,
Right in the nexte chapitre after this—
I gabbe nat, so have I joye or blis—
Two men that wolde han passed over see,
For certeyn cause, into a fer contree,
If that the wind ne hadde been contrarie,
That made hem in a citee for to tarie
That stood ful myrie upon an haven-side;
But on a day, again the even-tide,

54

The wind gan chaunge, and blew right as hem leste.
Jolif and glad they wente unto hir reste,
And casten hem ful erly for to saille.
But to that o man fil a greet mervaille: 310
That oon of hem, in sleping as he lay,
Him mette a wonder dreem again the day.
Him thoughte a man stood by his beddes side,
And him comanded that he sholde abide,
And seyde him thus: "If thou tomorwe wende,
Thow shalt be dreynt; my tale is at an ende."
He wook, and tolde his felawe what he mette,
And preyde him his viage for to lette;
As for that day, he preyde him to bide.
His felawe, that lay by his beddes side,   320
Gan for to laughe, and scorned him ful faste.
"No dreem," quod he, "may so myn herte agaste
That I wol lette for to do my thinges.
I sette nat a straw by thy dreminges,
For swevenes been but vanitees and japes.
Men dreme alday of owles and of apes,
And eek of many a maze therwithal;
Men dreme of thing that nevere was ne shal.
But sith I see that thou wolt heere abide,
And thus forslewthen wilfully thy tide,   330
God woot, it reweth me; and have good day."
And thus he took his leve, and wente his way.
But er that he hadde half his cours yseyled,
Noot I nat why, ne what mischaunce it eyled,
But casuelly the shippes botme rente,
And ship and man under the water wente
In sighte of othere shippes it biside,
That with hem seyled at the same tide.

And therfore, faire Pertelote so deere,
340 By swiche ensamples olde maistow leere
That no man sholde been to recchelees
Of dremes; for I seye thee, doutelees,
That many a dreem ful soore is for to drede.

Lo, in the lyf of Seint Kenelm I rede,
That was Kenulphus sone, the noble king
Of Mercenrike, how Kenelm mette a thing.
A lite er he was mordred, on a day,
His mordre in his avisioun he say.
His norice him expowned every deel
350 His sweven, and bad him for to kepe him weel
For traisoun; but he nas but seven yeer oold,
And therfore litel tale hath he toold
Of any dreem, so hooly was his herte.
By God, I hadde levere than my sherte
That ye hadde rad his legende, as have I.

Dame Pertelote, I sey yow trewely,
Macrobeus, that writ the avisioun
In Affrike of the worthy Cipioun,
Affermeth dremes, and seith that they been
360 Warninge of thinges that men after seen.
And forthermoore, I pray yow, looketh wel
In the Olde Testament, of Daniel,
If he heeld dremes any vanitee.
Reed eek of Joseph, and ther shul ye see
Wher dremes be somtime—I sey nat alle—
Warninge of thinges that shul after falle.
Looke of Egipte the king, Daun Pharao,
His bakere and his butiller also,
Wher they ne felte noon effect in dremes.
370 Whoso wol seken actes of sondry remes

May rede of dremes many a wonder thing.
Lo Cresus, which that was of Lyde king,
Mette he nat that he sat upon a tree,
Which signified he sholde anhanged bee?
Lo heere Andromacha, Ectores wyf,
That day that Ector sholde lese his lyf,
She dremed on the same night biforn
How that the lyf of Ector sholde be lorn,
If thilke day he wente into bataille.
She warned him, but it mighte nat availle;   380
He wente for to fighte natheles,
But he was slain anon of Achilles.
But thilke tale is al to longe to telle,
And eek it is ny day, I may nat dwelle.
Shortly I seye, as for conclusioun,
That I shal han of this avisioun
Adversitee; and I seye forthermoor,
That I ne telle of laxatives no stoor,
For they been venymous, I woot it weel;
I hem diffye, I love hem never a deel.   390
     Now let us speke of mirthe, and stinte al this.
Madame Pertelote, so have I blis,
Of o thing God hath sent me large grace;
For whan I se the beautee of youre face,
Ye been so scarlet reed aboute youre yen,
It maketh al my drede for to dien;
For al so siker as *In principio*,
Mulier est hominis confusio,—
Madame, the sentence of this Latin is,
"Womman is mannes joye and al his blis."   400
For whan I feele a-night your softe side,
Al be it that I may nat on yow ride,

For that oure perche is maad so narwe, allas,
I am so ful of joye and of solas,
That I diffye bothe sweven and dreem.'
And with that word he fley doun fro the beem,
For it was day, and eke his hennes alle,
And with a chuk he gan hem for to calle,
For he hadde founde a corn, lay in the yerd.

410 Real he was, he was namoore aferd.
He fethered Pertelote twenty time,
And trad hire eke as ofte, er it was prime.
He looketh as it were a grim leoun,
And on his toos he rometh up and doun;
Him deigned nat to sette his foot to grounde.
He chukketh whan he hath a corn yfounde,
And to him rennen thanne his wives alle.
Thus roial, as a prince is in his halle,
Leve I this Chauntecleer in his pasture,

420 And after wol I telle his aventure.

Whan that the month in which the world bigan,
That highte March, whan God first maked man,
Was compleet, and passed were also,
Sin March bigan, thritty dayes and two,
Bifel that Chauntecleer in al his pride,
His sevene wives walkinge by his side,
Caste up his eyen to the brighte sonne,
That in the signe of Taurus hadde yronne
Twenty degrees and oon, and somwhat moore,

430 And knew by kinde, and by noon oother loore,
That it was prime, and crew with blisful stevene.
'The sonne,' he seyde, 'is clomben up on hevene
Fourty degrees and oon, and moore, ywis.
Madame Pertelote, my worldes blis,

Herkneth thise blisful briddes how they singe,
And se the fresshe floures how they springe;
Ful is myn herte of revel and solas.'
But sodeynly him fil a sorweful cas,
For evere the latter ende of joye is wo.
God woot that worldly joye is soone ago;   440
And if a rethor koude faire endite,
He in a cronicle saufly mighte it write
As for a sovereyn notabilitee.
Now every wys man, lat him herkne me;
This storie is also trewe, I undertake,
As is the book of Launcelot de Lake,
That wommen holde in ful greet reverence.
Now wol I torne again to my sentence.

A col-fox, ful of sly iniquitee,
That in the grove hadde woned yeres three,   450
By heigh imaginacioun forncast,
The same night thurghout the hegges brast
Into the yerd ther Chauntecleer the faire
Was wont, and eek his wives to repaire;
And in a bed of wortes stille he lay,
Til it was passed undren of the day,
Waitinge his time on Chauntecleer to falle,
As gladly doon thise homicides alle
That in await liggen to mordre men.
O false mordrour, lurkinge in thy den,   460
O newe Scariot, newe Genilon,
False dissimulour, o Greek Sinon,
That broghtest Troye al outrely to sorwe.
O Chauntecleer, acursed be that morwe
That thou into that yerd flaugh fro the bemes.
Thou were ful wel ywarned by thy dremes

That thilke day was perilous to thee;
But what that God forwoot moot nedes bee,
After the opinioun of certein clerkis.
470 Witnesse on him that any parfit clerk is,
That in scole is greet altercacioun
In this mateere, and greet disputisoun,
And hath been of an hundred thousand men.
But I ne kan nat bulte it to the bren
As kan the hooly Doctour Augustin,
Or Boece, or the Bisshop Bradwardin,
Wheither that Goddes worthy forwiting
Streyneth me nedely for to doon a thing,—
'Nedely' clepe I simple necessitee;
480 Or elles, if free chois be graunted me
To do that same thing, or do it noght,
Though God forwoot it er that was wroght;
Or if his witing streyneth never a deel
But by necessitee condicioneel.
I wol nat han to do of swich mateere;
My tale is of a cok, as ye may heere,
That tok his conseil of his wyf, with sorwe,
To walken in the yerd upon that morwe
That he hadde met that dreem that I yow tolde.
490 Wommennes conseils been ful ofte colde;
Wommannes conseil broghte us first to wo,
And made Adam fro Paradis to go,
Ther as he was ful myrie and wel at ese.
But for I noot to whom it might displese,
If I conseil of wommen wolde blame,
Passe over, for I seyde it in my game.
Rede auctours, where they trete of swich mateere,
And what they seyn of wommen ye may heere.

Thise been the cokkes wordes, and nat mine;
I kan noon harm of no womman divine.   500

    Faire in the soond, to bathe hire myrily,
Lith Pertelote, and alle hire sustres by,
Again the sonne, and Chauntecleer so free
Soong murier than the mermaide in the see;
For Phisiologus seith sikerly
How that they singen wel and myrily.
And so bifel that, as he caste his ye
Among the wortes on a boterflye,
He was war of this fox, that lay ful lowe.
Nothing ne liste him thanne for to crowe,   510
But cride anon, 'Cok, cok!' and up he sterte
As man that was affrayed in his herte.
For natureelly a beest desireth flee
Fro his contrarie, if he may it see,
Though he never erst hadde seyn it with his ye.

    This Chauntecleer, whan he gan him espye,
He wolde han fled, but that the fox anon
Seyde, 'Gentil sire, allas, wher wol ye gon?
Be ye affrayed of me that am youre freend?
Now, certes, I were worse than a feend,   520
If I to yow wolde harm or vileynye,
I am nat come youre conseil for t'espye,
But trewely, the cause of my cominge
Was oonly for to herkne how that ye singe.
For trewely, ye have as myrie a stevene
As any aungel hath that is in hevene.
Therwith ye han in musik moore feelinge
Than hadde Boece, or any that kan singe.
My lord youre fader—God his soule blesse—
And eek youre mooder, of hire gentillesse,   530

Han in myn hous ybeen to my greet ese;
And certes, sire, ful fain wolde I yow plese.
But, for men speke of singing, I wol seye,—
So moote I brouke wel mine eyen tweye,—
Save yow, I herde nevere man so singe
As dide youre fader in the morweninge.
Certes, it was of herte, al that he song.
And for to make his voys the moore strong,
He wolde so peyne him that with bothe his yen
540   He moste winke, so loude he wolde cryen,
And stonden on his tiptoon therwithal,
And strecche forth his nekke long and smal.
And eek he was of swich discrecioun
That ther nas no man in no regioun
That him in song or wisedom mighte passe.
I have wel rad in "Daun Burnel the Asse,"
Among his vers, how that ther was a cok,
For that a preestes sone yaf him a knok
Upon his leg whil he was yong and nice,
550   He made him for to lese his benefice.
But certeyn, ther nis no comparisoun
Bitwixe the wisedom and discrecioun
Of youre fader and of his subtiltee.
Now singeth, sire, for seinte charitee;
Lat se, konne ye youre fader countrefete?'

    This Chauntecleer his winges gan to bete,
As man that koude his traisoun nat espie,
So was he ravisshed with his flaterie.

    Allas, ye lordes, many a fals flatour
560   Is in youre courtes, and many a losengeour,
That plesen yow wel moore, by my feith,
Than he that soothfastnesse unto yow seith.

Redeth Ecclesiaste of flaterye;
Beth war, ye lordes, of hir trecherye.

    This Chauntecleer stood hie upon his toos,
Strecchinge his nekke, and heeld his eyen cloos,
And gan to crowe loude for the nones.
And Daun Russell the fox stirte up atones,
And by the gargat hente Chauntecleer,
And on his bak toward the wode him beer,   570
For yet ne was ther no man that him sewed.

    O destinee, that mayst nat been eschewed,
Allas, that Chauntecleer fleigh fro the bemes,
Allas, his wif ne roghte nat of dremes,
And on a Friday fil al this meschaunce!

    O Venus, that art goddesse of plesaunce,
Sin that thy servant was this Chauntecleer,
And in thy service dide al his poweer,
Moore for delit than world to multiplye,
Why woldestow suffre him on thy day to die?   580

    O Gaufred, deere maister soverain,
That whan thy worthy King Richard was slain
With shot, compleynedest his deeth so soore,
Why ne hadde I now thy sentence and thy loore,
The Friday for to chide, as diden ye?
For on a Friday, soothly, slain was he.
Thanne wolde I shewe yow how that I koude pleyne
For Chauntecleres drede and for his peyne.

    Certes, swich cry ne lamentacion,
Was nevere of ladies maad whan Ilion   590
Was wonne, and Pirrus with his streite swerd,
Whan he hadde hent King Priam by the berd,
And slain him, as seith us *Eneydos*,
As maden alle the hennes in the clos,

Whan they had seyn of Chauntecleer the sighte.
But sovereynly Dame Pertelote shrighte
Ful louder than dide Hasdrubales wyf,
Whan that hir housbonde hadde lost his lyf,
And that the Romayns hadde brend Cartage.
600 She was so ful of torment and of rage
That wilfully into the fyr she sterte,
And brende hirselven with a stedefast herte.

O woful hennes, right so criden ye,
As, whan that Nero brende the citee
Of Rome, cryden senatoures wives
For that hir husbondes losten alle hir lives,—
Withouten gilt this Nero hath hem slain.
Now wole I turne to my tale again.

This sely widwe and eek hir doghtres two
610 Herden thise hennes crie and maken wo,
And out at dores stirten they anon,
And syen the fox toward the grove gon,
And bar upon his bak the cok away,
And criden, 'Out, harrow, and weylaway.
Ha, ha, the fox!' and after him they ran,
And eek with staves many another man.
Ran Colle oure dogge, and Talbot and Gerland,
And Malkin, with a distaf in hir hand;
Ran cow and calf, and eek the verray hogges,
620 So fered for the berking of the dogges
And shouting of the men and wommen eeke,
They ronne so hem thoughte hir herte breeke.
They yolleden as feendes doon in helle;
The dokes cryden as men wolde hem quelle;
The gees for feere flowen over the trees;
Out of the hive cam the swarm of bees.

So hidous was the noise, a, *benedicitee!*
Certes, he Jakke Straw and his meynee
Ne made nevere shoutes half so shrille
Whan that they wolden any Fleming kille,   630
As thilke day was maad upon the fox.
Of bras they broghten bemes, and of box,
Of horn, of boon, in whiche they blewe and powped,
And therwithal they shriked and they howped.
It semed as that hevene sholde falle.

   Now, goode men, I prey yow herkneth alle:
Lo, how Fortune turneth sodeynly
The hope and pride eek of hir enemy.
This cok, that lay upon the foxes bak,
In al his drede unto the fox he spak,   640
And seyde, 'Sire, if that I were as ye,
Yet sholde I seyn, as wis God helpe me,
"Turneth again, ye proude cherles alle,
A verray pestilence upon yow falle.
Now am I come unto the wodes syde;
Maugree youre heed, the cok shal heere abide.
I wol him ete, in feith, and that anon".'

   The fox answerde, 'In feith, it shal be don.'
And as he spak that word, al sodeynly
This cok brak from his mouth deliverly,   650
And heighe upon a tree he fleigh anon.
And whan the fox saugh that the cok was gon,

   'Allas,' quod he, 'O Chauntecleer, allas,
I have to yow,' quod he, 'ydoon trespas,
In as muche as I maked yow aferd
Whan I yow hente and broghte out of the yerd.
But, sire, I dide it in no wikke entente.
Com doun, and I shal telle yow what I mente;

I shal seye sooth to yow, God help me so.'
660   'Nay thanne,' quod he, 'I shrewe us bothe two.
And first I shrewe myself, bothe blood and bones,
If thou bigile me ofter than ones.
Thou shalt namoore, thurgh thy flaterye,
Do me to singe and winke with myn ye;
For he that winketh, whan he sholde see,
Al wilfully, God lat him nevere thee!'
    'Nay,' quod the fox, 'but God yeve him
      meschaunce,
That is so undiscreet of governaunce
That jangleth whan he sholde holde his pees.'
670   Lo, swich it is for to be recchelees
And necligent, and truste on flaterye.
    But ye that holden this tale a folye,
As of a fox, or of a cok and hen,
Taketh the moralite, goode men.
For Seint Paul seith that al that writen is,
To oure doctrine it is ywrite, ywis;
Taketh the fruit, and lat the chaf be stille.
Now, goode God, if that it be thy wille,
As seith my lord, so make us alle goode men,
680   And bringe us to his heighe blisse! Amen.

THE NUN'S PRIEST'S
EPILOGUE

'Sire Nonnes Preest,' oure Hooste seide anoon,
'I-blessed be thy breche, and every stoon,
This was a murie tale of Chauntecleer.
But by my trouthe, if thou were seculer,
Thou woldest ben a trede-foul aright.
For if thou have corage as thou hast might,
Thee were nede of hennes, as I wene,
Ya, moo than seven times seventene.
See, whiche braunes hath this gentil preest,
So gret a nekke, and swich a large breest,   690
He loketh as a sperhauk with his yen;
Him nedeth nat his colour for to dyen
With brasile, ne with greyn of Portingale.
Now, sire, faire falle yow for youre tale!'

  [And after that he, with ful merie chere,
Seide unto another, as ye shuln heere.]

NOTES

At the point at which we enter upon the story of the pilgrimage, the Monk has been delivering a few of the hundred short stories that he has copied out, all of which bear upon the tragedy of human life. It had been expected that he would deliver a single narrative and since there is no sense of construction or unity in his stories beyond their pessimistic mood he is halted by the Knight and the Host.

1–3. Although it was agreed that the Host of the Tabard Inn, Southwark, Harry Bailly, should act as general compère for the entertainment, it is the Knight and not the Host who interrupts the Monk and opens the Prologue. The Knight is courteous, though his phrase, *and muchel moore* ('and a good deal too much'), is distinctly impatient.

5–7. Here the speaker begins a recapitulation of the Monk's prescription for tragedy. The Host also quotes from the Monk. It may be noticed that lines 5–24, which contain these echoes, are missing from roughly half of the existing manuscript versions of the poem. We may interpret this as follows. The shorter version contains everything that is essential to the Introduction of the next Tale whereas the longer one pauses to recapitulate what has gone before. It would seem that the longer version was composed for use when Chaucer had decided upon his final order and was ready with a piece that we might term an interchapter which connected two tales firmly together. The Monk's definition of tragedy will be found on p. 10.

12. *it thinketh me* The first of several impersonal verbs used in the poem. It means 'as it seems to me' with the object in the dative case.

14. St Paul's Cathedral, London.

16. The phrases between quotation marks come from *The Monk's Tale*, which ends

> And covere hire brighte face with a clowde.

The Host pretends not to understand its meaning which is 'how fortune keeps the uncertainties of the future hidden', or possibly 'how fortune suddenly changes, like the sun going behind a cloud'.

18–19. The words *biwaille* and *no remedie* also echo the Monk. The speaker has a good memory.

22. The Host is echoing the Knight here.

25. *desport ne game* A demand for amusement above all else is another repetition of the Knight's idea that 'litel hevinesse is right ynough to muche folk'.

28–9. *nere clinking...* 'were it not for the clinking of your harness bells'. The Monk has been described as a celebrated horseman and the bells on his harness sounded *as loude as dooth the chapel belle* (i.e. too loud). His name, Dan Piers, is given at this point for the first time, which may be taken as evidence that Chaucer was still modifying his framework-poem while he was busy with the individual tales.

31. *for sleep* 'to sleep'. Great care must be exercised in the translation of certain prepositions and conjunctions. Lines 181, 343, 351, 533, 606, 620 and 724 will provide more examples; see also the note to line 51.

35–6. 'If a man has nobody to listen to his story there is no point in his speaking at all. And I know I have the making (of an attentive listener) in me if a tale is well told.' Cf. note to lines 16–19 above. Chaucer often shows, however, that the Host misunderstands what he has heard.

39. The Monk loved hunting, though this was inappropriate to his calling. The Host is getting in a sly dig here.

42–9. There is no respect evident here in his use of 'thou Sir John' or in the remarks about the wretchedness of his horse. Sir John was a familiar name for any priest in the Middle Ages and it is an open question whether this was his proper name or not. It reappears on the last line of the Prologue.

50–1. 'Yes, Host, as I hope to go (on horseback or on foot) I know I shall be criticized if I do not tell a merry story.' In this sentence, which shows the Priest rather squashed by all that has been said to him, the word *but* means *unless*. This is an example of a conjunction that must be carefully weighed before rendering into Modern English.

The first 25 lines of this Tale are memorable and among the finest poetically in the whole work. Chaucer does not often proceed in such depth as he does here. Since his narratives were generally designed for recitation aloud it was best not to have them composed in a style that hampered immediate understanding. A listener, after all, cannot turn back again to

re-read a passage. However, there are so many individual words
that repay particular attention that we may single them out
while realizing that the original listeners would not have done so.
The anonymous widow, for instance, is associated with words
like *sklendre, narwe* and *litel,* though they are not directly
attributed to her. The overtones of *n'apoplexie* and *no wyn,* for
example, redound to her credit since she triumphed over poverty
with moral excellences. Her poverty and patience are those
practised by the religious orders, and her dietary (not a special
diet in the modern sense) is nourishing but plain. The reader
may turn up the essay on this Tale by David Holbrook in *The
Pelican Guide to English Literature,* vol. I, for a more detailed
reading of this verse-paragraph.

55. *stape* 'advanced'; another manuscript reading, *stoupe,*
    which conveys the old woman stooping through age, is not to
    be ignored. It might be said that the ideal would be to convey
    both meanings at once.
61. *catel* and *rente* Terms expressing 'capital' and 'income'.
    They are both too grandiose for the small sums involved and
    this is part of the poet's technique of ironic degradation used
    throughout the first page of the story.
63. *she foond hirself* 'she provided for herself'; cf. line 78.
66. This line immediately calls up the mock-heroic manner.
    The customary use of *bour* and *halle* to describe a two-roomed
    cottage is far removed from the other, courtly, connotation of
    bower and hall, knights and fair ladies. It was *sooty* because
    it was of the traditional pattern and had a central fire with
    the smoke finding its way out through a hole in the roof.
    The *yerd* outside is a parody of the moat outside a medieval
    castle.
68. *hir neded never* 'she never needed'. The construction is
    again an impersonal one, literally 'it was never needed to
    her'.
70. 'Her diet was in keeping with her cottage.'
71–2. 'She was never sick through gross over-eating; the
    moderation of her diet was medicine enough for her.'
74–5. 'She was not prevented by the gout from dancing nor was
    her head ever harmed by apoplexy.' Both diseases can be
    caused by over-eating and drinking.
76–7. *whit* and *reed* wines, placed in contrast with *whit* and
    blak, milk and rye bread. The four negatives that are

given in line 76 remind us that two, three and four negatives
will be found in close conjunction in medieval writings without their cancelling each other out. In verse especially the
insertion of an extra negative particle helps in filling out the
metrical pattern.

80. *a maner deye* 'a kind of dairy maid'. The meaningless *as it
were* is a further example of the poet working with the demands
of the metre and with the aural expectations of his listeners.
The reader will find numerous examples of phrases and
similes brought in, especially for the purposes of rhyme, which
also allow a second in which the audience did not have to
concentrate fully upon the unfolding of the Tale. These
phrases also give the impression of natural speech, which is
full of such redundant elements.

84–98. The richness of the portrait of Chauntecleer contrasts
startlingly with that of his human mistress. This has the
effect of emblazoning him upon our imagination and exposing
his greater self-consciousness. It is essential that the widow
should be described first so that her simplicity should act as a
foil for this portrait. He is associated with the furnishings of a
church (85–8); with music (84–8); with a medieval fortification
(94); with command over outer space (89–92) and several of
the strongest colours (93–8). He is everything that is powerful,
vigorous and positive, where the widow is retiring, typical
rather than individual, and best characterized in a passage full
of negatives.

85–6. *orgon* This word was plural in Middle English perhaps
because it consisted of keyboard and a set of pipes or because
it needed a player and blower to make it sound. To perform on
a medieval organ was a formidable undertaking, rather like
playing on a carillon, which needs considerable force. (The
word *gallows* is similarly plural today although it is singular in
image.) *gon*, play (plural).

87. 'His crowing in his lodge (i.e. his perch) was more reliable
than any clock.'

89–90. 'He knew the passing of time and the circle of the
heavens by instinct.' Each *ascencioun* of the *equinoxial* or hour
was measured by the movement of a circle drawn in the
sky immediately above the equator. Medieval astronomers
supposed that there was a measure by which it was possible to
judge the angle of the earth's inclination towards or away from
the sun, an angle that increased or decreased by fifteen degrees

an hour. For further information upon medieval astronomy, see
An Introduction to Chaucer, chap. 6.

94. *batailled* 'battlemented'. Compare the associations of
bour and *halle* described in the note to line 66 above. In his
own eyes Chauntecleer was worthy of such a superb analogy.

95–8. The colours are magnificent but conventional. It has
been pointed out that they are the colours of ecclesiastical
vestments, as if Chauntecleer symbolized the priesthood.
These colours were to be found in the armour of Henry
Bolingbroke, shortly to become Henry IV, who was personally
known to Chaucer. If we resist such special identifications the
descriptions are realistic or detailed enough for an American
scholar to identify the breed as the Golden Spangled Hamburg,
a progenitor of the modern Brown Leghorn cock. It has more
recently been pointed out that this species has tufts or 'beards'
(see line 154) and that they look graceful and attractive
enough at the early age of a week to substantiate the comment
on Pertelote at line 107.

101. The seven hens must be both 'sustres' and 'paramours'.
The line makes it difficult for us to accept Chauntecleer as the
symbol of the good but negligent human soul—as has been
claimed by some writers—and still less the good but negligent
priest. To accept the symbolic interpretation one has to
swallow an uncomfortable amount of realistic detail. The
sexual element has now entered the poem: *plesaunce* in the
preceding line is one of the causes of his undoing.

105–7. Pertelote (Partlet) is revealed in terms befitting the
mistress of a prince and in continued contrast with those
reserved for the human performers in this drama. Even so,
she is given far less space than her husband and is later made
to react in the manner of a middle-aged housewife. The
burnished colours of the Cock's portraiture resemble the
manner of description associated with a medieval heroine rather
than a hero. Vigour and force are expected of a male rather
than colourfulness.

108–10. 'She had subdued Chauntecleer, held him fast in
heart and limb. He loved her so much that perfect happiness
seemed to be his.'

113. A popular song of the period: 'My love has gone away'.

116 ff. From this moment the Tale begins in greater earnest.
At once Chaucer catches the tone of a human dialogue for his
two speakers. We find this in the conversational ease of 'his

wives alle' or 'this faire Pertelote' and 'this Chauntecleer'. We are made to sense that we are all listening to a recitation not too far away from the fire in the centre of a hall in which the birds are perching at this moment. From this point onwards we may pay attention to the breathless tone of the narrative passages and the number of lines and even paragraphs that open with the word *And*.

121. 'As a man who is greatly perturbed in a dream.'

122 ff. From this moment the couple establish themselves in our imagination as man and wife. He is sick and rather cowardly, she is practical and solicitous. We forget the other six sister-wives and concentrate on the interplay of two quite different minds.

125. 'What a sound sleeper you are!' (ironical).

127. *ye take it nat agrief* 'don't be alarmed'.

128. *meschief* 'trouble'. *me mette* is impersonal here and at lines 132 and 312. The reader is advised to note the form of this verb carefully.

130. *recche aright* 'interpret correctly' (i.e. bring to a happy ending). Another MS reading equally helpful is *rede aright*.

134. *maad areest* 'made a snatch at my body'.

136–8. The colours mentioned in these lines call forth Pertelote's oratory on the subject of the four bodily humours. The speaker nowhere uses the word 'Fox', so it may be assumed that he had no name for him, had never seen one and that the central episode of this Tale is a completely fresh experience. Cf. line 515. There is a certain absurdity in his describing a Fox so clearly and yet evoking an elaborate misinterpretation of the dream.

142. *Avoy* The heroine in the episode from *Le Roman de Renard* on which Chaucer may have based this Tale uses the same exclamation at this point, but another MS of the Priest's Tale gives *Away* instead.

hertelees 'coward'.

148. See the entry under *fraunchise* in *An Introduction to Chaucer*, p. 188. In *The Shipman's Tale* we read that husbands are to be 'hardy, and wise, and riche, and therto free'.

150. 'Nor a man who is afraid of every weapon.' Impressions of the Cock's cowardice and fear multiply throughout the first half of the Tale. He is a changed character at the end when he plots his own happy escape, showing no fear at all as he is borne along in his enemy's mouth.

154. The beard is human in so far as the subject of the address is interpreted as a human, but see note to lines 95–8.

156. *vanitee* 'emptiness'.

157 ff. The view here of the interrelation of dreams and humours is a faithful reflexion of what was held in the Middle Ages on these matters. The Introduction, pp. 13–18, examines the subject in greater detail.

161–70. *superfluitee* (too much) of any single physiological element in the body's make-up throws it off balance. This is still valid and obvious but Pertelote then improvises. She is aware that the four humours in the body were blood, phlegm, choler and black bile, and she associates red objects like arrows with fiery tails and red-hot coals with the red humour, choler. Similarly she argues from black bile and melancholy that this must be the humour in excess causing her husband to see black images. *Contek* and *whelpes* convey no colour image. She comes nearest to the truth without fully realizing it when she says:

> Or elles blake develes wole hem take.

In this line it is the moral association of the colour that counts.

172. 'That make many a man full of sorrow in his sleep.'

174. *Catoun* is the author of *Disticha Catonis*, a popular school-book of the Middle Ages. His full name was Dionysius Cato and Chaucer uses his authority on other occasions. The exclamation *Lo Catoun!* is a formula used in medieval debates when an authority is cited. The poem now assumes the structure of a disputation with each speaker presenting a viewpoint.

175. *ne do no fors* 'pay no heed to'. She cites his idea correctly.

177. *as taak* 'please take'.

178. *up peril* 'on peril'.

183–4. 'I shall teach you what herbs will be to your greatest advantage and benefit.'

186–7. 'Which have the natural properties of easing you through vomiting or excretion.'

189. *coleriok of compleccisun* 'choleric by disposition'.

190. 'Beware of (becoming overheated in) the sun at its zenith.'

192. *leye a grote* 'bet fourpence'.

195–9. These are all genuine herbal cures of the day: *lawriol*, a dark evergreen laurel; *centaure*, a member of the gentian family; *fumetere*, fumitory; *ellebor*, a poisonous emetic;

katapuce, and *gaitris beryis* are also purges prescribed, like everything else in Pertelote's list, for stomach ailments. *Herbe ive* is less easy to identify. The *wormes,* natural food for a hen, were also prescribed by Dioscorides especially for tertian fevers in humans.

200. *mery is* 'is so delightful'. While this phrase is clearly inserted for the rhyme, it gives a lilt and buoyancy to the whole passage in which Pertelote warms to her task. One senses her excitement in the poetry and this culminates in the fine, vigorous line:

> Pekke hem up right as they growe and ete hem in.

202. *fader kin* Not an empty appeal to his father's line; see the passage on that father by his killer, lines 536–45.

203. *I kan sey yow namoore* At the end of this torrent of advice is a nice touch of characterization.

204. The courtesy of this rejoinder (*graunt mercy,* 'many thanks') is a way of disposing of an inferior's argument by a counter-appeal to different authorities. Chauntecleer is on his dignity.

210. *so moot I thee* 'as I hope to prosper', a common imprecation.

211. 'That maintain exactly the opposite of his opinion.'

217. 'Experience amply proves this to be the case.'

220. *in a ful good entente* 'with the holiest of intentions'. The first example from Chauntecleer's dream-lore acts upon the reader with a startling immediacy. It shows a series of warnings which, going unheeded, prove too late. Both Cicero in *De Divinatione* and Valerius Maximus in *Facta et Dicta Memorabilia* related incidents similar to this and the example that follows. Cicero would have been the authoritative name to wield in a debate but it seems that Chaucer obtained his material from an English adapter, Robert Holkot, in *Libri Sapientiae.*

223. *streit of herbergage* 'short of accommodation'.

227. *departen* 'part'.

229. *as it wolde falle* 'as chance decided'.

231. *fer in a yeerd* 'a good distance away down the farmyard'.

233. *aventure or his fortune* 'chance or luck'. The element of ill-luck is magnified until it brings about a much more significant issue: whether human actions are determined by God or are completely free.

239. *ther I lie* 'where I lie'.

242. 'The man woke out of his sleep with a start of fear.'

244. *no keep* 'no attention'.

245. *vanitee*, one of the notable words of this Tale, is picked up from line 156. To fasten a point in a debate back upon a word in the opponent's case is a useful way of scoring a trick.

250. *morwe tide* 'morning time'. *Tide* here as in 'Whitsuntide'.

254. 'Have that cart stopped without hesitating.'

264. *your felawe is agon* This has a double meaning: 'your companion has left' and 'your companion has departed this life'.

266. 'This man became suspicious.' *Gan* is not to be translated 'began to' when it is followed by an infinitive: it is a way of expressing the past tense. This word occurs several times in the Tale and must be carefully translated.

268. *no lenger wolde he lette* 'he would delay no longer'.

276. *gaping upright* 'flat on his back with his mouth open'.

278. *sholden* 'ought to'.

280. *what sholde I?* 'why should I?'.

281. *out sterte* 'rushed out'. In some MSS this is given as *upsterte*.

283. *al newe* 'very recently'.

286. *mordre wol out* 'murder will reveal itself'. This phrase is also heard in *The Prioress's Tale* when a body is thrown in a dung-pit.

287–91. The word *abhominable* at first sight appears to derive from *ab homine* (away from a man, unmanly) though it correctly derived from *abominari* (turn away from evil omens). Even so, Chaucer seems to have accepted the first interpretation. One interesting fact attaches to this passage in the Tale. In one of the most reliable manuscripts the word *auctor* (the author) appears in the margin, usually interpreted as the poet's own addition to any authority he had been citing. The moralization and 'this my conclusioun' may as a result have a firmness as from Chaucer himself rather than from either the Priest or the Cock.

292–6. The *ministres* use torture to extract a confession, and deal summary justice. Their counterparts in *The Prioress's Tale* acted similarly and with a zeal which spilled over into revenge against innocent victims. It is possible that this incident is a comment by the Priest upon his superior's Tale, since the two Tales are related, especially in the passage following about Kenelm (lines 344–53).

298 ff. The second main example from Chauntecleer's dream lore is a single warning received too late and its tragedy is

succinctly and almost briskly narrated to add to the effect of pity. This example like the last would befit *The Monk's Tale* but the total effect of the present tale is not upon this level.

306. *again the even-tide* 'towards evening'. *Again, agains* and *against* (cf. line 312) were interchangeable.

312–14. *him mette...him thoughte...him comanded* The first two are impersonal verbs taking the dative case, while the third is used in the active voice with a direct object.

319. *as for that day* 'just for that day'.

322–3. 'No dream', he said, 'will disturb me so much that I will let my business affairs slip.'

330. 'And thus hang about and lose time.'

335. 'By accident the ship's bottom was stove in.' The line is stark and bald, offering no explanation at all of the mystery.

343. 'Many dreams are to be feared most strongly.' Chauntecleer must be judged to have made his point in the debate. His later experience adds further irony to the statement because he nowhere compares the troublesome dream with the animal who appears to tempt and waylay him.

344–53. The example of the child-saint Kenelm is a sidelong glance at the life of the Christian child in the ghetto told earlier to the pilgrims by the Prioress. Kenelm succeeded to the throne of Mercia in Britain in 821. His ambitious elder sister named Cwenthryth had him murdered. His dream was of climbing a tree which was cut down, releasing his soul to fly away. His nurse interpreted it for him as a portent.

348. *say* 'saw'.

351. *for traisoun* 'against treachery'.

352–3. 'His heart was so pure that he attached little importance to any dream.' His trusting nature was not aroused to suspicion.

354. 'I would give my shirt for you to have been able to read this legend as I myself have.' A brilliant example of the humour to be derived from the confusion of animal and human images. It is happening early in the morning and it is tempting to imagine a husband walking round in his shirt before breakfast.

357–60. Scipio Africanus Minor is said to have had a dream in which his grandfather foretold the outcome of a Carthaginian siege. Cicero's fictional *Somnium Scipionis* describes this dream, and a further commentary upon it is that by Macrobius in the fourth or fifth century A.D. Chaucer depicts himself reading this book at the opening of *The Parliament of Fowls*, a work that deserves comparison with *The Nun's Priest's Tale*.

361–71. Chauntecleer turns to the Bible for the brief examples or *exempla* which follow. Turning to the scriptures to back up a case was a necessary part of the technique of the contemporary sermon. Here it intensifies the narrative. Daniel vii ff. and Genesis xxxvii and xl–xli are the references for these incidents. The latter, together with Scipio's dream, is mentioned in Chaucer's *Book of the Duchess*.

370. *actes* here means 'notable events'.

372–4. The investigation now turns to classical legends for material. The dream of Croesus forms the last paragraph of *The Monk's Tale*. He dreamt he was in a tree receiving the attentions of the gods and this was interpreted as a premonition of his hanging. The fact that the Nun's Priest repeats the incident has been seen by some writers as proof that the present order of tales was an afterthought. It probably only proves that Chaucer liked the story, which he found in *Le Roman de la Rose*, one of his favourite French books.

375–82. The dream of Andromache, Hector's wife, was a medieval addition to the Troy legend, lacking the authority of Homer. However, it is unlikely that Chaucer or anybody else troubled about the authenticity of what was a useful example of premonition.

386–90. 'I shall suffer some adversity from the vision.' He refers once more to his own dream. He refuses the proffered laxative, giving only the petulant reason, 'I mistrust them, I do not like them at all'. This is a very weak conclusion after so impressively argued a case, but it is also quite human to refuse medicines on the grounds of taste and after-effects.

388. 'I have no faith in laxatives.'

391. *stinte al this* 'stop all this'. The phrase recalls the first line where the Knight changes the Monk's subject with a similar command.

391–408. This passage is richly human and comic. After so much biblical and classical allusion the scholarly bird comes to the love scene. The satire upon human endearments suits a celibate narrator with a dislike of the women in his immediate neighbourhood. The revelation of the difficulties confronting a mating pair whose quarters are too restricted underlines that humanity still more heavily. However, we notice that

Chauntecleer is off upon the pursuit of biblical sentiments yet again, quoting to suit his own purposes and taking advantage of his wife's ignorance, or displaying his own, by offering a completely inaccurate translation. *In principio* ('In the beginning') is the opening of Genesis and St John's Gospel. *Mulier est hominis confusio* means 'woman is man's ruin'. The passage may have come to Chaucer from one of his favourite authors, Vincent de Beauvais, whose *Speculum Historiae* was one of the popular books of universal chronology from the time of the Creation onwards. Reference to the Creation immediately reminds the reader that woman was man's ruin at the time of Adam and Eve, but that since he loved her he was beguiled and accepted a portion of the blame. The irony comes back upon Chauntecleer like a boomerang. He knows all about dream-portents and he despises Pertelote's wifely advice, but when the onslaught comes he is no more equipped to deal with it than she would have been. One of his faults is pride, another pedantry; still further it is uxoriousness, or being subdued by his wife because of his passion for her—in this case *womman* (or a hen) is *mannes joye and al his blis*, and the cause of his *confusio* as well. It is the human problem of Original Sin and the confusion of sex and other responsibilities that the Nun's Priest is discussing in his fable.

405. It is not certain that Chaucer had a consistent differentiation between *sweven* and *dreem*, so that the line is untranslatable.

407. *his hennes* is the subject of *fley doun* in the previous line.

412. *prime* 6 a.m. according to the Church's time-table. Chauntecleer has been voted more reliable than the church-clock. At line 456 it is *undren* or 9 a.m.

415. *him deigned nat* 'he did not deign'. The verb (an impersonal one) conveys pride: he is a royal creature, a lion almost, but one susceptible to the cunning of the fox.

419. *pasture* is one of the words in the Tale which has most notably altered in meaning since the Middle Ages. Here it means the act of feeding and not the ground which provides food for cattle.

421–31. This is a highly complicated passage, partly a satire upon the over-complex modes of calculation adopted by astronomers of the period. March is made the starting-point because it was the start of the year in the medieval calendar. It either means that 32 days after 1 March, which is 1 April, the events depicted took place, or that they took place on 3 May (when March was complete, and 32 days had *also* passed). It has often been recalled that Chaucer used the same date for that moment in *The Knight's Tale* wherein Palamoun broke out of prison, and in *Troilus and Criseyde* where Pandarus persuades his niece Criseyde to receive Troilus.

427–33. Having established the date as a precise and unlucky moment in the annual round, Chaucer now turns back to do it again not through the months of the year but through the signs of the zodiac which were associated with them. The zodiac was a belt which seemed to contain the movements of the celestial bodies and it was divided into a dozen segments each of thirty degrees. Each of the segments was a lunar month and each degree a day. The sign of Taurus (April/May) follows the sign of Aries, the Ram, which was in the ascendant at the moment when Chaucer imagined the opening of his masterpiece:

> and the yonge sonne
> Hath in the Ram his halve course yronne.

Both Aries and Taurus are symbols of strong masculinity and the latter suits the present context, one male with seven females, very well.

433. The satire on astronomy continues. Whereas the previous reckonings have established the date by two methods, this passage refers to the time of day, 9 a.m. Although the mathematical calculations with their 'and one and somewhat more' look exceptionally tentative it is the angle of elevation for the sun on 3 May, and not 1 April.

434–8. One bird is patronizing his smaller brethren: a revelation of pride and another human failing. The heavy rhyming throughout these lines is a way of conveying the pomposity through sound-effect alone. At the opening *my worldes blis* we are ready to watch out for the after-effect of his admission of his sexual passions and it follows at line 438, *a sorweful cas.* This small passage captures the purpose of a much lengthier section of the poem: 'a dreadful accident immediately befell him'.

441–3. 'If a rhetorician could compose elegantly enough he might put this into a chronicle as a supreme example.' It is intended as an example of the transience of earthly joys and as a gibe at the rhetorical principles of Geoffroi de Vinsauf; see pp. 24–7.

446–7. Sir Launcelot, hero of one of the Arthurian romances where he is the lover of Queen Guinevere, is judged by the narrator to be suitable only for woman readers avid for stupid fiction. *That* may refer either to the hero or the book.

448. The promise to return to the original narrative, repeated from line 420, reminds us how little of the story has yet been told although we are past the half-way mark. Satire on diffuseness of story-tellers grows by pointing out the number of digressions.

449 ff. The introduction of a *col-fox*, one with black coloration on ears and tail, answering exactly to the dream-figure, though not explicitly recognized, sends the story on to a renewed sense of urgency. The title given to this fox has caused speculation in recent years. J. L. Hotson, the Shakespearean scholar, has explained that Colfax was a surname in Chaucer's time and that Nicholas Colfax, a man of *sly iniquitee*, might well have been in the author's mind. He had assisted in the assassination of the Duke of Gloucester in Calais in 1397, the event referred to at the opening of Shakespeare's *Richard II*. If the Tale was written after the murder one can hardly see how it would fail to have acquired this meaning or how this could not have been the poet's intention. We also know that Chaucer had reasons for hating the dead Duke, an unpopular man who in 1386 had deprived Chaucer of his offices of profit under the Crown. Unfortunately we have no way of dating the Tale and it would beg the question to date it as late as 1397–8 merely on this coincidence.

450. *woned yeres three* 'lived three years'. There is no reason for his living there three years, a number full of symbolic suggestion to allegorists; still less for Chauntecleer's not having met him before.

451. *heigh imaginacioun* 'divine foreknowledge'. Since a long discussion of divine foreknowledge is shortly to come, this interpretation seems preferable, although 'vivid imagination' has also been proposed.

458. *homicides* That the fox and Colfax should both be murderers fits Hotson's theory perfectly.

459. *in await* 'waiting for'.

460–3. Three traitors mentioned here combine to form a nice fusion of the great literature of the day. *Scariot* is Judas, the betrayer of Christ; *Genilon* is Ganelon who betrayed the forces of King Charlemagne in *Le Roman de Roland*; while Sinon advised the Trojans to admit the Trojan Horse which let the Greeks secretly into Troy prior to their capture of the city. The point of these figures is that they are so inappropriate as analogies to a farmyard incident.

464–5. 'May this morning when you flew down from the beams into the yard be always accursed.'

467–84. At last the dream is vindicated as prophetic and not the result of stomach disorder. This leads into a difficult passage in which Chaucer takes a light-hearted but well-informed look at theological issues of the day, those over which there was 'greet altercacioun'. On line 475 the views of St Augustine, bishop of Hippo, in his *De Civitate Dei*, are mentioned. His idea was that although God had foreknowledge of human lives, this in no way deprives man of his freewill. On line 476 Chaucer turns to his favourite philosopher, Boethius, whose *De Consolatione Philosophiae* he translated into English. The views of 'Boece' are more difficult to summarize but they try to combine foreknowledge and freewill in this fashion: that God knows in advance that actions will take place but does not know exactly when, or the chain of causes that will lead towards them. Bradwardine was archbishop of Canterbury for a short time before his death in 1349, and his study of the problem is contained in *De Causa Dei*. His viewpoint, similar to the more familiar and later Calvinism, is that God has such foreknowledge and control over man. It is unnecessary to define the poet's own viewpoint. He was assembling these views, putting them side by side and suggesting that if experts disagree others cannot possibly know how to think. He also makes the controversy ridiculous by placing it in the context of an animal fable.

474–5. 'I cannot sift the wheat from the chaff' or 'I cannot make head or tail of it.' The verb *kan* in these two lines deserves special attention. It means 'know how to', 'am able to' and 'am allowed to'. An explanation of this ambiguity is to be found in the variety of speakers this passage may be assumed to have. First of all it is Chauntecleer, then the Nun's Priest, last Chaucer himself. Since this is a theological issue it may be assumed that the cock and the layman find it too difficult: they are not able to unravel the complexities because they have not the special knowledge. None of the three is

presented as professional theologian and it is only a university theologian who is competent to decide on these issues;
even the Priest is without the full understanding. Finally,
none of these is *allowed* to pronounce on these matters
because they are the preserves of the corporate body of
Church theologians under the control of the pope. On the
next line we find that Augustine *kan*: he is able to, knows how
to and is allowed to because he is a highly respected divine,
and so are the other scholars; but the trouble is that those who
kan do not agree.

477–84. This passage is still highly technical. 'Whether God's
foreknowledge that commands our respect forces me of
necessity to perform an act (I may term this "simple necessity")'—Bradwardine's theory. 'Or whether free choice is
given to me to perform or not to perform that act, even
though God had known of it in advance'—Augustine's
theory. 'Or whether his foreknowledge has only a conditional
power over my act'—Boethius's theory. This is a précis
rather than a suitable translation.

484. *but* 'except'.

490–3. A return to the topic of sex also raises the subject of
Original Sin and the Garden of Eden. In human terms this is
to remind us of the problems arising from the Fall; in
animal terms it may refer to the popular belief that in Eden
there was perfect amity between the different beasts and no
fox would attempt to waylay a cock. The extent of the changes
introduced by the conventional idea of the Fall is in keeping
with all the discussions of predestination and theology re-
corded in the lines above.

495–6. Making a serious matter into a *game* when it becomes
controversial is a typically Chaucerian amusement. So too is
his request that a reader shall impute anything he may dislike
to the imaginary narrator rather than the poet himself. On
line 499 he offers one of these disclaimers which tie readers
logically up in knots and incline us to dismiss the whole as a
joke.

500. The meaning, most probably, is 'I know nothing dis-
creditable to women'. Here the word *kan* is to be interpreted
as 'know'. But everything else from the narrator discredits
this statement.

501. There are less than 200 lines to go and the tempo of
narrative is accelerating at last.

505. *Phisiologus* refers to a popular study of animals known as the bestiary in which natural history combines with examples of unnatural history. To equate Pertelote with a deceptive mermaid is certainly unfair. The essential innocence of all the hens is conveyed in words such as *faire* and *myrily*: to proceed from this state to a sharp criticism of the sex is to go beyond the evidence of the narrative.

510. 'He had no desire at that moment to crow.'

515. 'Though he had never seen it at all before.' Our impression at this moment is of a man in a primal state of innocence not yet introduced to the element of evil in his nature and the universe.

521. *wolde harm* 'intended harm'.

522. 'I have not come here to spy on you and your plans.'

528. Boethius, one of Chaucer's favourite philosophers, also wrote a work *De Musica* which reduced music more to mathematical ratios and geometrical proportions than actual musical harmonies. The book had nothing to say about the natural music of birds and the effect of the reference is to reduce a Platonic study to a baser reality, a further example of the mock-heroic principle of the poem.

531. The couple met their deaths in the Fox's house, though his allusion is naturally ambiguous, and richly ironic.

533. *for men speke of singing* 'on the subject of singing'.

534. 'As I hope to enjoy the use of my two eyes.' The irony here is that he immediately suggests that Chauntecleer should close his two eyes (at lines 539–40) to facilitate the attack.

540. *winke* 'keep eyes closed'.

546–53. Burnellus the donkey is the hero of a Latin poem entitled *Speculum Stultorum* written by a twelfth-century monk from Canterbury named Nigel Wireker. In the episode under discussion a young man broke the leg of a chicken who later took his revenge. While the youth Gundolf was studying for the priesthood the bird crew so late that he caused his former tormentor to oversleep on the very morning that he was due to present himself for a church benefice and his prospects were ruined. The whole book is a satire on the Church and a suitable source of quotation for the Nun's Priest to draw upon. Line 553 *his* refers to Wireker's cock.

555. 'Let us see how well you can imitate your father.' The speaker means that Chauntecleer shall follow his father all the way to the Fox's dinner-table.

559–64. This moralization for an imaginary audience seems to refer to another sermon. Ecclesiasticus xxvii. 26 or Proverbs xxix. 5 provide the correct quotation.

568. The name Russell means 'red one' and it appears in *Le Roman de Renard* as that of Reynard's son. J. L. Hotson has claimed that it also identified the fox with Sir John Russell, one of the courtiers of Richard II. See note to line 449.

569. It is completely appropriate that the victim is taken by the throat. The presiding Sign, Taurus (l. 428) was astrologically associated with Head, Neck and Shoulder. See M. Hussey, *Chaucer's World*, p. 22.

571. *sewed* 'pursued'.

572–608. The final rhetorical flourish in which the hand of destiny is traced back to the gods, and Venus is attacked for not protecting her subject Chauntecleer even on her name-day. The discussion of Christian theories of predestination is made to look still more absurd by reverting classical myths at the fateful moment. Friday (in French *Vendredi*) has been considered a day of omen, whether through the association with Venus, or the Norse goddess Frig who presides over the day in Northern mythology or through the crucifixion of Christ on Good Friday. All such interpretations of the day's significance are ridiculed in these lines of rhetorical address.

579. The teaching of the Church upon human conception—that sexual intercourse must be directed solely towards the conception of a child—is made ludicrous by association with a cock, seven hens and the pagan goddess of love.

580. *woldestow* 'should you'.

581. Here Chaucer names Geoffroi de Vinsauf, whose rhetorical principles aided him throughout the composition of the poem. He is the *rethor* to whom reference was made on line 441 and the passage upon the death of Richard I was a celebrated extract from his book, *Nova Poetria*. See Introduction, pp. 24–7.

584–5. 'Why was I not endowed with all your sentiments and learning to be able to utter a complaint against Friday as you did?' Richard I was wounded on Friday 26 March 1199.

590–4. *Ilion* Troy; *Eneydos*, *The Aeneid*. The lamentations of woman reviewed here resemble the far larger collection in Dorigen's complaint in *The Franklin's Tale*. Once more there is a distancing, mock-heroic effect gained from the immediate context. A batch of clucking hens is not an impressive form of

Greek chorus to strike the full tragic pity and terror into the audience.

591. *Pirrus* Pyrrhus who killed Priam, the Trojan ruler, and took away Andromache, Hector's widow.

streite swerd 'drawn sword'.

597. Hasdrubal was ruler of Carthage when it was burned down by the Romans in 146 B.C. The story of his wife's suicide was probably found by Chaucer in Vinsauf's *Nova Poetria*, the source of the lament upon Richard I. The same story appears as part of the comparable passage in *The Franklin's Tale*:

> when she saugh that Romayns wan the toun,
> She took her children alle and skipte adoun
> Into the fyr.

In that extract too one can detect a mock-heroic intention in the words *skipte adoun*.

603–8. This final classical example also appeared in *The Monk's Tale*.

607. 'Nero put them all to death though they were innocent.'

609 ff. The climax is reached at last in a passage of magnificent action poetry where the images are only of a farmyard, and unadulterated with irrelevant learning. Chaucer's handling of the familiar contemporary scene with animals, people and all the noise imaginable brings forward the positive interest of the poet and the audience in contemporary life.

611. It will be noticed that this line, like six others very close to it, gains its breathless vigour and movement by its syntax: the conjunction *And* starts each line off at a furious pace. Such a chase was well known in the pictorial art of the period and Chaucer had the task of suiting the vivacity of comic picture with the appropriate verbal energy.

617. *Colle oure dogge* is not necessarily a collie dog. The other two names were given to hunting dogs. *Oure* does not denote possession but a deep involvement in the subject and a way of giving it immediacy.

620. 'Very frightened because of the barking of the dogs.'

622. *breeke* 'broke'.

623. The devil symbols here have suggested to some critics that the incident is to be taken as a counterpart of the Fall. Paradise symbolism has indeed been encountered in the Tale but its effect is never serious and it fails to lift the story on to the highest plane of seriousness. It might be thought that the

writer had another pictorial idea in his mind, that of the devils in the paintings of hell or possibly those in the hell scenes in the mystery plays.

624–5. 'The ducks cried out as if the men were killing them; the geese flew away over the trees in their fear.'

628. Jack Straw and his fellows were associated with the Peasants' Revolt of 1381 when the mob rose up against the government and demanded more favourable terms of taxation. Flemings in London were persecuted and killed during the rising. These were workers in the cloth trade, men from Ypres and Gaunt who were the rivals of the Wife of Bath. Chaucer uses this image as his only concession to contemporary history.

632–3. Note the alliteration here. *Bemes*, 'trumpets'; *box*, 'boxwood'.

635. This carries on the train of thought from line 623 and intensifies it.

636. *goode men* The narrator seems to lapse into the formula proper to a sermon congregation. He does it again at line 674.

637. The address or apostrophe to Fortune seems to make a mockery of all the discussion of predestination. After citing theologians he turns to the pagan concept of Fortune for his moral.

641–2. 'Sire, if I were in your place, I would say, as surely as (I hope) God may help me, ...'

646. *Maugree youre heed* 'in spite of everything you can do'.

658. Another sardonic offer.

663–4. 'You shall no more flatter me into singing with my eyes shut.' Chauntecleer has profited from the chastening experience.

668. *undiscreet of governaunce* 'so lacking in self-control'. The moral is equally applicable to both actors in this episode: one sees human failings in each. It remains now for the Priest to elaborate rather enigmatically on the meaning of this entire fable.

672. *folye* Animal tales and the like were condemned by some members of the Church as lacking in decorum and dignity.
     But ye 'but you who'.

674. What exactly is the moral of the tale? It is not the same to every modern reader. See pp. 34–40 where it is discussed more fully.

675. St Paul makes this remark in Romans xv. 4: 'whatever was written in former days was written for our instruction'.

677. *Fruit* and *chaf*, images drawn from harvesting. The meaning is still elusive because of Chaucer's habit of taking the ground away from under our feet when we believe we have penetrated to the serious application of the fable. In *Parliament of Fowls* Chaucer makes a similar statement:

> For out of olde feldes, as men seyth,
> Cometh al this newe corn from yer to yere,
> And out of olde bokes, in good feyth,
> Cometh all this newe science that men lere.

679–80. The conclusion is in keeping with the speaker's profession, but *Amen* is also to be found at the end of *The Miller's Tale*, where it denotes an ending rather than a serious moral purpose. Nobody has been able to discover the identity of 'my lord' but he may have been a bishop or the archbishop. It remains another enigma.

The Epilogue is not found in all MSS of the Tale but it is genuine.

681–6. The tone here is disrespectful to the Priest as a priest but it is a compliment to him as a man and a 'manly man', large and boisterous. The Host suggests a link between the story and the speaker's convent background and recognizes it as a projection of his own situation. *Trede-foul*, a cock in the act of copulation; *corage*, 'sexual prowess'. For the revelations to be found in this passage, see Introduction, pp. 5–10.

691. *sperhauk* 'sparrow-hawk'. The bird imagery from the Tale is extended to the teller.

692–3. 'He has no need to dye himself with red dye (from brazil wood) or Portuguese cochineal grain.'

694. 'May you prosper for telling us so good a story.'

695–6. The last couplet is barely acceptable and is held to be a copyist's effort to effect a transition into the following story, that of the Second Nun. It has been thought that the Epilogue as a whole may have been rejected by Chaucer once he had written the Prologue to *The Monk's Tale* which also makes speculations about the teller's virility.

BOOKS FOR FURTHER READING

The following books will give the reader some further critical assistance with this Tale:

T. W. Craik, *The Comic Tales of Chaucer* (Methuen, 1964).

Boris Ford (Ed.), *The Age of Chaucer* (Pelican, 1954).

Charles Muscatine, *Chaucer and the French Tradition* (California University Press, 1957).

John Speirs, *Chaucer the Maker* (Faber, 1951).

Trevor Whittock, *A Reading of Canterbury Tales* (Cambridge University Press, 1968).

GLOSSARY

abhominable unnatural,
  hateful (see note to l. 287)
abreyden wake up with a
  start
accord harmony
accordant to in keeping with
adversitee difficult
  circumstance
aferen frighten
afferment verify, state
affrayen frighten
again towards (period of
  time)
agasten frighten
agrief amiss
agu ague, acute fever
al quite; (l. 463) very
als also
altercacioun wrangling,
  disputation
amenden equal, better
anhangen hang
anon immediately
anoyen weary
apothecarie chemist, druggist
areest arrest, restraint
arrayen prepare, get ready
arresten stop
arwe arrow
ascencioun rising above the
  horizon; (l. 190) zenith
asure azure blue
attamen begin
attempree moderate,
  temperate
auctor author
avauntour boaster, braggart
aventure chance, luck

avisioun dream, vision
avoy alas
bad (inf. *bidden*) bade
bane death
bar (inf. *beren*) behaved
batailled battlemented,
  crenellated
beer (inf. *beren*) bore
beme beam; (l. 632) trumpet
bene bean, worthless object
benedicitee (pr. *bencité*) God
  bless us
benefice church living
berd beard
bere bear
berking barking
beth (inf. *ben*) be
biden wait
bifel (inf. *bifallen*) it happened
biknewe (inf. *biknowen*)
  confessed
bile bill
bitwixe between
biwaillen bewail, lament
biwreyen reveal
blisful happy; (ll. 431, 435)
  blessed
blithe gay, joyous
bole bull
boon bone
boterflye butterfly
botme bottom
bour bower, bedroom
box boxwood
brak (inf. *breken*) escaped
brasile red dye obtained from
  brazil-wood
brast (inf. *bresten*) burst

braune muscle
breche breeches
bren bran
brend (inf. *brennen*) burnt
bridde bird
brouken enjoy the use of
bulten sift, bolt
burned burnished
butiller butler
cas chance, mischance
casten resolve, plan
casuelly by accident
catel property, chattel
centaure centaury
certes assuredly, certainly
cherle slave, fellow
chiden reproach, complain
chukken cluck
clappen babble
clepen call
clerke scholar
clomben (inf. *climben*) climb
cloos closed, shut
clos enclosure, yard
colde fatal
colera, colere, colerik choler,
    choleric humour
col-fox fox with black
    markings
commune in common,
    commonly
compaignable friendly,
    sociable
compleccioun temperament
condicioneel conditional
conseil advice; (l. 522)
    secrets
contek strife
contrarie natural enemy
contree country
coomb comb
corage sexual vigour

corn grain of corn
cote cottage
cours voyage
curteys courteous (see
    An Introduction to Chaucer,
    p. 188)
damoisele damsel, mistress
Daun Master
debonaire gracious, pleasant
deel part, piece
deigne (inf. *deynen*) deign,
    condescend
delit pleasure
deliverly smartly, deftly
departen divide, part
    company
desport sport, entertainment
devisen describe, relate
deye keeper of a dairy
deyen die
deyntee delicate
diffyen challenge, mistrust
discrecioun discernment
discreet prudent, judicious
disese displeasure
disputisoun debate
dissimulour dissembler
distaf distaff, a cleft stick
    used for winding wool
divinen suppose (see note to
    l. 500)
doctrine teaching
doghtren daughters
donge dung
doutelees certainly
drecchen distress, vex
drede fear
dreynt (inf. *drenchen*)
    drowned
ech each
eek also
eeris ears

91

eet (inf. *eten*) ate

ellebor black hellebore

elles else

enditen compose, write

Eneydos The Aeneid by Virgil

engendren cause, start

enginen put on the rack

ensample example

entente intention

equinoxial time at which sun
   crosses equator and day
   and night are equal

er, erst before

eschewen avoid, evade

ese pleasure

espyen catch sight of

estaat condition, social
   standing

everemo for ever

everichon everyone

experience observation,
   practice

expownen expound

ey egg

eylen be wrong with, ail

fader father

fain willingly, gladly

faren travel, go

feend devil, fiend

felawe friend, companion

fer far

fetheren copulate (of birds)

fil (inf. *fallen*) befell

flatour flatterer

flaugh (inf. *fleen*) flew

fleen fly; (l. 513) escape

fleigh, fley (inf. *fleen*) flew

folye silly thing

foond (inf. *finden*) found;
   (ll. 63, 78) provided

forncast forecast

fors, no no problem

forslewen lose through
   delaying

forwiting foreknowledge

forwoot (inf. *forwiten*) knows
   in advance

foryet (inf. *fory(g)eten*) forget

free generous (see
   An Introduction to Chaucer,
   p. 188)

fro from

ful very

fume vapour

fumetere fumitory

fy! fie!

gabben tell a lie

gaitris beryis buckthorn

game sport, fun

gan (inf. *ginnen*) began;
   frequently used to form
   past tense

gapen open mouth wide

gargat throat

Genilon Ganelon, betrayer
   of *Chanson de Roland*

gentillesse nobility, courtesy
   (see *An Introduction to
   Chaucer,* p. 188)

gessen guess, suppose

gilt sin

gladen make glad, cheer

gladsom delightful,
   pleasant

gooth (inf. *goon*) went

governaunce control; (l. 668)
   self-control

greve grove

greyn cochineal dye

gronen groan

grote groat = fourpence

habundant abundant

han (inf. *haven*) have

harrow! cry for help

haven-side shore of a haven
heele health
heer hair
heeren hear
heet (inf. *heten*) was called
hegge hedge, fence
heighe high, exalted
helen conceal
hem them; (l. 111) him
henten seize, catch
herbe-ive herbive, coronopus
herbergage harbourage, accommodation
herknen listen
hertely sincerely
hevinesse seriousness, grief
hewed coloured
hider hither
highte (inf. *heten*) is called
hir, hire their; (l. 68) her
hostelrye inn
hostiler innkeeper
homicide murderer
hoo! stop!
hoold keeping
housbondrie economy
howped (inf. *houpen*) whoop
humour mood, state of mind (see *An Introduction to Chaucer*, ch. 6)
Ilion Troy
iniquitee wickedness
jade miserable horse, nag
janglen chatter
jape jest, trick
jeet jet
jolif jovial, cheerful
kan (inf. *konnen*) can, knows how to
katapuce catapuce
keen kine, cows
kepen watch over

kinde nature, natural properties; (l. 430) instinct (see *An Introduction to p. Chaucer*, 189)
konnen be able to, know how to (see note on l. 155)
koude (inf. *konnen*) could
ladde (inf. *leden*) led
lak shortage
lat (inf. *leten*) let
lawriol spurge laurel
laxatif laxative
leere (inf. *leren*) learn
leme flame
leoun lion
lesen lose
leste (inf. *lusten*) it pleased
leten stop, prevent; (ll. 268, 323) delay; (l. 318) postpone
levere rather
liggen lie
lite little (of time); *gret and lite* of all types
lith limb; (l. 502) lies (vb.)
logge lodging
loggen lodge
loken (inf. *louken*) lock
londe, in far away
loore wisdom, teaching
lorn (inf. *losen*) lost
losengeour deceiver, flatterer
lust inclination
maad (inf. *maken*) made
maistow mayest thou
malencolye melancholy
maugree in spite of; *maugree youre heed* in spite of all you can do
maze fancy, delusion
meschaunce, mischaunce mishap

93

meschief trouble

messedayes mass-days for laymen

met, mette (inf. *meten*) dreamt (see note to l. 128)

meynee followers

ministre magistrate, office

mirthe fun, merriment

mooder mother

moot may; *moot I thee* as I hope to thrive

moralitee moral lesson

mordre murder

mordrour murderer

morwe, morweninge, morwe-tide morning

mosten must

muche, muchel many, much

murie merry, pleasing

namo, namoore no more

narwe narrow

nas (= *ne was*) was not

nathelees none the less

necligent negligent

nedely necessarily

nere (= *ne were*) were it not

nice foolish

nigard miser

nones, for the for the time, occasion

noon none

noot (= *ne woot*) know not

norice nurse

notabilitee noteworthy fact, idea

ny near

o one

ofter oftener

orgon organ

orlogge clock

outrely utterly

out-sterten rush out

paramour mistress

pardee by God, certainly

parfit perfectly

pasture feeding

pekken peck

peril, up on peril

pestilence plague

peyne trial, ordeal; (l. 588) suffering

peynen take pains, exert oneself

pinen torture

pitous deplorable, piteous

plesaunce pleasure

pleyen amuse, jest

point detail

povre poor

poweer, al his his utmost

powpen blow, toot

poynaunt sharp-flavoured

preeve practical test

prime six a.m.

prively secretly

propretee quality, attribute

prow benefit, advantage

purgen relieve, clear

quellen kill

quod (inf. *quethen*) said

rad (inf. *reden*) read

rage frenzy

real royal, regal

recchelees careless, imprudent

recchen interpret

rede red

rekken care, heed

reme realm

remenant remainder

rennen run

rente revenue

repaire go frequently (to)

repleccioun over-eating; (l. 157) excess of humour

repleet overfull

rethor rhetorician

reulen govern

revel merrymaking

revers contrary, opposite

rewen be sorry

riden mount

roghte (inf. *rekken*) heeded

romen walk up and down

ronne (inf. *rennen*) ran

roore (inf. *roren*) roared

rude rough, hasty, tactless

saufly safely, confidently

saugh (inf. *seen*) saw

Scariot Judas Iscariot

scole university

scornen ridicule

secree discreet

seculer layman

seinte holy

sely innocent, simple, good, humble

sentence subject-matter; (l. 211) opinion; (l. 399) meaning

sewen pursue

seyen say

seyn (inf. *seen*) seen

seynd smoked

shaltow shalt thou

shente (inf. *shenden*) injured

sherte shirt

shrewen curse

shrighte, shriked (inf. *shriken*) shrieked

shrille shrill

shul (v. *shall*) shall

sik sick

sikerer more sure, regular, trustworthy

sikerly surely

sith since

sklendre slender, scanty

slawen (inf. *sleen*) slain

slough swamp, puddle

smal slender, slim, narrow

sodeyn sudden

solas solace, delight

somdeel somewhat

sone; sonne son; sun

soond sand

soong (inf. *singen*) sang

soore grievously; (l. 293) sorely; *ful soore* greatly to be dreaded

sooth truth

soothfastnesse truth

sovereyn, sovereynly supreme, supremely

spak (inf. *speken*) spoke

sperhauk sparrow-hawk

springen rise

stalle shed

stape advanced

stave stick

stedefast constant, unwavering

sterten start

stevene voice

stikke stake

stinten stop

stirte (inf. *sterten*) jump

stoon testicle

streit limited, restricted; (l. 591) drawn

streynen constrain

substaunce essential element

subtiltee cunning, ingenuity

suffisaunce contentment

superfluitee excess

suspecioun suspicion

sustre sister

swevene dream

swich such

syen (inf. *seen*) saw
tarien delay
terciane fever fever which
   grows only on alternate
   days
thee (inf. *theen*) prosper
thilke that
tho those
thogh though
thridde third
thritty thirty
thurgh through
tide time
tiptoon tiptoes
tool weapon
toon, toos toes
tornen return
touching regarding
trad (inf. *treden*) trod,
   copulated with
traisoun treason
trede-foul treader of hens
   (= cock)
trespas wrong
trewe true
tweye two
twies twice
undertaken give one's word
undiscreet lacking
undren forenoon
vanity vain thing; (l. 156)
   illusion
venyme poison
verray true, actual; (l. 125) fine
viage voyage
vileynye villainy, low
   behaviour (see *An Introduc-*
   tion to Chaucer, p. 190)
voys voice
war aware
waren beware
weel well

wenden go
werken cause
wexen grow, become
weylaway! alas!
whatso whatsoever
whelpe dog
wher that (ll. 365, 369)
whilom once
widwe widow
wight person, man
wikke evil
winke close the eyes
wis surely
witing knowledge
wlatsom ugly
wode wood
wonder strange
wonen dwell
wook (inf. *waken*) awoke
woot (inf. *witen*) know
worte vegetable
worthy divine
wroght (inf. *werken*) done,
   made
yaf (inf. *yeven*) gave
ybeen (inf. *ben*) been
ydoon (inf. *doon*) done
ye yes; (ll. 507, 515) eye
yeerd, yerd yard, enclosure
yen eyes
yeven give
yfounde (inf. *finden*) found
ygon (inf. *goon*) gone
ylogged (inf. *loggen*)
   accommodated
ynough enough
yollen yell
yronne (inf. *rennen*) run
yseyled (inf. *seylen*) sailed
ywarned (inf. *warnen*) warned
ywis certainly
ywrite (inf. *writen*) written